Heartw
LONDON

Heartbeat
LONDON

MICHAEL ELLIOTT

FIRETHORN PRESS

First published in Great Britain in 1986 by
Waterstone & Co. Limited
49 Hay's Mews
London W1X 7RT

Firethorn Press is an imprint of
Waterstone & Co. Limited

British Library Cataloguing in Publication Data

Elliott, Michael
    Heartbeat London: the anatomy of a supercity.
    1. London (England) – Social life and customs – 20th century
    I. Title
    942.1085'8   DA688

    ISBN 0 947752 62 5

Typeset in Melior by Type Generation, London
Printed and bound in Great Britain by
Billing & Sons Ltd
Worcester and London

TO EMMA

PREFACE

This book reflects one person's view of London, but it could not have been written without the help and encouragement of many others. The book grew out of a survey published in *The Economist* in January 1986, and my first debt is to Gordon Lee, *The Economist*'s surveys editor. He suggested London as a topic; spotted that my work might make a book; and then introduced me to Heather Holden-Brown, who started as a publisher and ended as a friend. My second debt is to her and everyone else at Firethorn Press who made working on the book so enjoyable.

Other colleagues at *The Economist* helped enormously. Simon Jenkins' extraordinary knowledge of London was always a resource placed willingly at my disposal; Andrew Knight and Rupert Pennant-Rea, editors of the paper during the time the book was written, both smiled benignly on the project. Frances Cairncross, my editor on the Britain section of *The Economist,* did much more. She could easily have been intolerant with what must have been constant red-eyed tetchiness on my part; instead, she egged me on, and was almost as excited when the proofs arrived as I was. Richard Natkiel Associates – old friends of *The Economist* – prepared the maps.

Among the scores of people I badgered for information for both survey and book, special mention must be made of those GLC officials who, through publications or in person, provided so many facts and figures. Future authors will not find an enterprise like this easy now the GLC is gone.

And then there are my friends and relations, whose lives I plundered shamelessly for my own purposes. To them, both thanks and apologies for boring them with London for most of a year. None bore that with greater fortitude than my wife; without her support not a word of the book would have been written.

Michael Elliott
London, *April 1986*

vii

CONTENTS

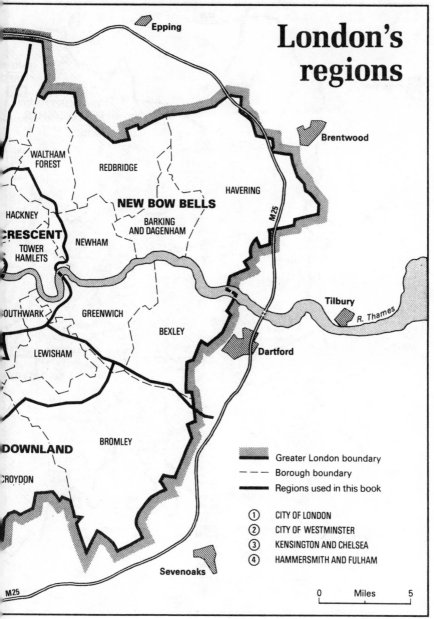

London's regions

Epping

Brentwood

WALTHAM FOREST

REDBRIDGE

HAVERING

NEW BOW BELLS

HACKNEY

CRESCENT

BARKING AND DAGENHAM

M25

TOWER HAMLETS

NEWHAM

SOUTHWARK

GREENWICH

Tilbury

R. Thames

BEXLEY

Dartford

LEWISHAM

DOWNLAND

BROMLEY

CROYDON

Sevenoaks

M25

Greater London boundary

Borough boundary

Regions used in this book

① CITY OF LONDON
② CITY OF WESTMINSTER
③ KENSINGTON AND CHELSEA
④ HAMMERSMITH AND FULHAM

0   Miles   5

xi

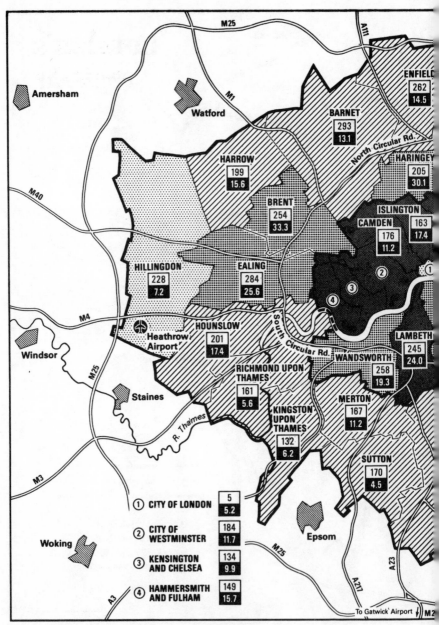

Amersham

Watford

M25

M1

ENFIELD
262
14.5

A111

BARNET
293
13.1

North Circular Rd.

HARROW
199
15.6

HARINGEY
205
30.1

M40

BRENT
254
33.3

ISLINGTON
163
17.4

CAMDEN
176
11.2

② ①

HILLINGDON
228
7.2

EALING
284
25.6

③

④

M4

Windsor

M25

Heathrow
Airport

HOUNSLOW
201
17.4

South Circular Rd.

LAMBETH
245
24.0

WANDSWORTH
258
19.3

Staines

RICHMOND UPON
THAMES
161
5.6

MERTON
167
11.2

R. Thames

KINGSTON
UPON
THAMES
132
6.2

SUTTON
170
4.5

M3

① CITY OF LONDON
5
5.2

② CITY OF
WESTMINSTER
184
11.7

Epsom

M25

A23

Woking

③ KENSINGTON
AND CHELSEA
134
9.9

④ HAMMERSMITH
AND FULHAM
149
15.7

A217

A3

To Gatwick Airport

M2

xii

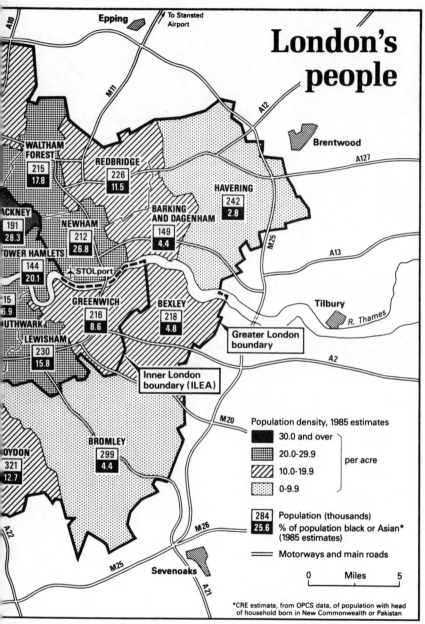

London's people

Epping

To Stansted Airport

Brentwood

A127

WALTHAM FOREST
215
17.8

REDBRIDGE
226
11.5

HAVERING
242
2.8

ACKNEY
191
28.3

NEWHAM
212
26.8

BARKING AND DAGENHAM
149
4.4

A12

M25

A13

A13

TOWER HAMLETS
144
20.1

STOL port

15
6.9

GREENWICH
216
8.6

BEXLEY
218
4.8

Tilbury

R. Thames

UTHWARK

LEWISHAM
230
15.8

Greater London boundary

A2

Inner London boundary (ILEA)

M20

M11

A10

Population density, 1985 estimates

■ 30.0 and over
▦ 20.0-29.9
▨ 10.0-19.9
▫ 0-9.9

per acre

BROMLEY
299
4.4

ROYDON
321
12.7

284
25.6
Population (thousands)
% of population black or Asian*
(1985 estimates)

═ Motorways and main roads

A22

M26

M25

Sevenoaks

A21

0   Miles   5

*CRE estimate, from OPCS data, of population with head of household born in New Commonwealth or Pakistan

xiii

1
MORE A COUNTRY THAN A CITY: INNER LONDON

This book is about a great city, and what makes it great. Yet how do you describe a city? How, in particular, do you describe a city that has had an importance for 2,000 years, which was for many of those years the world's most populous metropolis, and yet which is often said (and has been said for at least three centuries) by those who live in it or comment on it to be no more than a collection of villages?

At least one recent book was tempted to give up the unequal struggle: "Does London exist?", it asked in the first paragraph, and concluded that it did, but only just. Yet that tag of the "city of a hundred villages" is only one way of looking at London, and arguably not the best one. Though Londoners may well say that they live in Hampstead, or Battersea, or Romford, or Richmond, they will also say that they live in London. It is too romantic by half to pretend that the city is entirely constructed on the small scale. London's property market is well developed, and its population a mobile one; young Londoners might well live in four or five different parts of the city before they settle down. Village loyalty means that Londoners like the places that they live in – indeed, one of the city's most endearing characteristics is that it has so many pleasant places to make a home – it does not mean that London cannot be considered as a unity.

Another modern writer has got much closer to the truth. "London is not a city. It is more like a country, and living in it is like living in Holland or Belgium. Its completeness makes it deceptive – there are sidewalks from one frontier to the other – and its hugeness makes it possible for everyone to invent his own city. My London is not your London, though everyone's Washington, DC is pretty much the same." Put to one side the established chroniclers of London – Dickens, Jonson, Johnson and Betjeman. Those words in the delightful novel *The London Embassy* by the American writer Paul Theroux catch the flavour of the modern city nicely, and give an introduction to its importance.

The 610 square miles that make up the political entity of London have a population of more than 6.7m. That is bigger than Switzerland, Denmark, Bolivia, New Zealand or a city-state like Hong Kong. London's economy dwarfs that of plenty of countries who worry the world's bankers and commentators. Within living memory, it was the biggest commercial centre that the world had ever seen, and the capital and administrative hub of a huge Empire. Yet to approach London as a country is difficult. Its whole being is so wrapped up with a genuine country – Britain – that it is hard to treat London as it deserves.

Let us try. Consider first London's history. Granted, there is little evidence of any settlement in London before the Romans, and there were other Roman towns whose importance rivalled London's. But London thrived during the first four centuries after Christ, and though it fell into disrepair after the Romans' final departure in 410, it was almost certainly the nation's largest city long before the Norman conquest over 600 years later. It has never been of anything other than the first importance since then, and there is a sense in which London's history has made Britain's history, not the other way round. But a country must have more than a history. It must have a geography as well – a set of regions each of which has a distinct unity. So what are the regions of our imaginary country of London?

First, forget the 32 boroughs, and the City of London (the area that roughly delineates the original Roman settlement) whose boundaries make up those 610 square miles. The boroughs have only been political units for 20 years, when they, and the Greater London Council (GLC), a directly elected "strategic" local authority that had some responsibilities in all the boroughs' areas, were created. The GLC was abolished on March 31st this year. The boroughs are still there, but their boundaries tell one little about the social geography of London. Forget, even, the 610 square miles. A tourist's "London" is much smaller than that; an economist's much bigger. For some, "London" is literally no more than a few streets round their house. A friend of mine once met with blank looks when, at an adult education class, she used a tube map as a visual aid. None of her students knew what the tube was. For others, "London" is just a junction in a web of international contacts; a place from which businessmen whizz down telephone lines or flightpaths (Heathrow is the world's busiest international airport) to London's suburbs in New York, Paris or Tokyo.

Leave those extremes aside. To find your way around the real London, pretend that its map is divided into ten regions, four making up what Londoners refer to as "inner London" (though we do not use that term in its precise political meaning – ten boroughs and the City which together make up the Inner London Education Authority, an administrative area with about 2.5m people) and six in "outer London". For fun, I have invented my own names for them, as well as their boundaries. You won't find them identified on any maps other than the ones at the front of this book, but you should be able to work out which region you're in quite easily. Inner London first.

Park and City
This is central London, a mis-shaped rectangle bounded on the south by the River Thames from Chelsea to the Tower; the City Road from the Tower to Islington to the east; the Marylebone Road and then the urban motorway known as the Westway to the north; and on the west, by

roads that run through Earl's Court to the river at Chelsea.
Area, about 12 square miles; population just over
400,000. It includes within it the twin cities of London
and Westminster (the City graduated from its Roman
origins to be the financial and commercial heart of
London; from pre-Norman times, Westminster was, as it
remains, the seat of government), and most of the Royal
Borough of Kensington & Chelsea. Within its borders is
some of the world's most valuable real estate. Rents for
new property in the heart of the City can reach more than
£35 a square foot, on the City's borders a little less. In the
West End – an area that includes the new retail
extravaganza in Covent Garden, the fleshpots of Soho,
and St James's and Mayfair, the bolt-holes of old money –
rents are around £30 a square foot, sometimes more.

Salaries in this area can come pretty high too. Brokers
in the money markets can gross £500,000 a year. Top
lawyers in the Temple, just west of the City, can earn as
much. The new entrepreneurs and the old aristocrats of
the West End earn sums that only heaven and their
accountants know. Most people in Park and City,
naturally, do not have great wealth or anything like it, but
those who do give the place some of its flavour. This is
where you see the Rolls-Royces (rare in Britain outside
London); the swish expense account restaurants where a
meal might cost £80 a head; the night-clubs and casinos
where money appears to be no object. Predictably, prices
of residential property are sky-high. Though there are
parts of Park and City where you could buy a
two-bedroomed flat for £60,000, they are few and far
between. To buy a house you would have to go way over
£100,000. In Belgravia, parts of Kensington or the housing
estate north of Hyde Park, the home of your dreams might
cost £500,000 to £1m.

None of this means that all the population of Park and
City is wealthy. The main reason it isn't is the British
pattern of public – or council – housing. The borough of
Westminster has 32% of its dwellings publicly owned;

Kensington & Chelsea, which has a smaller proportion of public housing than any of the "inner London" boroughs, still has 26% of its dwellings housing families who pay rent to its council. The consequence of this mixture of wealth and public housing is that almost every area of Park and City has a mixture of inhabitants. Take, as one example, Pimlico, once a red-light district behind Victoria Station. In the 1950s, the children of the big houses in Belgravia, across the Buckingham Palace Road from Pimlico, moved into its cheap nineteenth-century flat-fronted houses. (They might have paid ground rent to the same landlord – the Duke of Westminster – as their parents. The Westminsters, however, had sold Pimlico in 1950.) But Pimlico has plenty of public housing, by no means all of it old, so that its shopping streets have a pleasant atmosphere of shoulder-rubbing between the great and the not-so-great. The same is true of Covent Garden, where council estates and housing association blocks are tucked in behind the old warehouses, full of loft conversions. Chelsea is similar; a big public housing estate occupies one of the choicest spots in town, just where the King's Road comes closest to the river.

It would be naive, and inaccurate, to say that all of central London's people enjoy the same things. Britain remains a class-bound society; London has not escaped that curse. But on one matter all Londoners agree. The city's parks give it a flavour that is utterly unique among the world's great towns. You can start walking in Holland Park, at the north-west corner of Park and City, move south-east, cross Kensington Church Street to Kensington Gardens, enter Hyde Park, use the underpass into Green Park, cross in front of Buckingham Palace into St James's Park, and arrive at the Houses of Parliament having walked four miles. Of that walk, all but a short stroll through Kensington will be on grass. If walking strains your heart, take a cab to the Albert Hall. Stroll north-east a few hundred yards until you come to a bridge over the Serpentine, Hyde Park's lake. Look east, to Big Ben; turn and look west, to the 278-foot high spire of St Mary Abbots, Kensington. There are few views in the heart of the country that give the impression of such a sylvan landscape.

Yet the green of London does not depend only on its parks. The rich families who owned and built its centre – of whom the Westminsters were the richest – had taste. Sometimes, it almost seems as if their developments were a conscious effort to mimic within a city the feeling of space they had in their country estates. And thus came London's squares, hundreds of them. The white squares of Kensington and Belgravia are perhaps the best known, but all of Park and City has them. Try Bloomsbury (though note that London University has ruined some of the most elegant squares of all); try Hanover Square, tucked behind Oxford Street, with its splendid church (St. George's), guarded by two cast-iron sculptured hounds; try Fitzroy Square, in the delightful village just west of the Tottenham Court Road that its inhabitants call Fitzrovia. Almost anywhere in central London, a short walk will take you to a square – although not all of them are open to the public – where you can escape a fair part of the city's bustle.

It goes without saying that Park and City is the region of London that tourists know. For many, indeed, it is the only part they ever see, for two reasons. The first is that all the tourist attractions are in Park and City. The art galleries are there; the theatres, the palaces, the Tower, the museums in South Kensington, the cathedrals and churches. The second reason is equally important. Park and City is hotel country. Over half of the beds in London's hotels, guest-houses and bed-and-breakfasts are in Westminster and Kensington; add to them the cheaper accommodation in Bloomsbury (within the borough of Camden) and it is a strange tourist indeed who does not spend his nights sleeping in Park and City.

It is not only the tourists that give Park and City its international feel. The City is the most outward-looking part of the whole British economy; its earnings from overseas increased from £1.3 billion in 1975 to £3 billion in 1981, and doubled again to more than £6 billion by 1984. Some lawyers have cashed in on the fact that much of the world seems to love a British court: the most aggressive have now diversified their practices into European and world markets. Even the education service looks abroad for its earnings. The London School of Economics & Political Science ("the LSE", to those who have had little to do with it; "the School" to those who have) has been so busy attracting foreign students for the past five years that its hideously crowded building just off Fleet Street now feels like an Ivy League campus without the grass. And, of course, there are the theatres. The exchange rate of the dollar against the pound is the most important variable in show-business; more than 40% of West End theatre tickets are now sold to foreigners.

The same pursuit of foreign currency can be seen among London's retailers. An analyst for a leading estate agent recently worked out a precise correlation between the tourist trade and rents on Oxford Street. As tourist numbers went up, so, a year later, did rents. Newer retail areas like Covent Garden are full of stores that make a direct pitch for the tourist. Older ones, like Knightsbridge, sometimes seem to be populated entirely by foreigners. Harrods (owned by Egyptians) and Harvey Nichols are, and have been for years, international stores, not just British, much less London, ones.

The foreign influence on the retail trade has served London well. It has brought a new set of goods into the shops, and priced them competitively. Even more important, it has had beneficial side effects on the conservation of London's fabric. Since 1970 there has been hardly a single act of major vandalism on old buildings in Park and City, and this is at least partially because of the influence of tourists. They love to find modern shops behind nineteenth-century – or earlier – facades. Without the promise of the tourist trade, the old fruit and vegetable markets in front of Inigo Jones's piazza in Covent Garden would have been torn down. The success of refurbishment there means that the next great development – probably on the site of the Smithfield meat market to the north of the City, arguably an even finer building than Covent Garden – will be similarly preserved.

But there is no denying that some of the effects of the internationalisation of London have been less happy. The flood of Arab money into Park and City after the first oil shock in 1973 helped an already overheated property market to boil over; first-time house buyers are still counting the cost. Victoria, with its coach and train stations disgorging tens of thousands daily, looks a tacky mess for most of the year, and is unbearable in summer. Queensway, to the north of Hyde Park, turns itself into a Middle Eastern souk on Friday nights. The newsagents sell Arabic papers; the shops sell sticky sweets; the street walkers wear djellabis – and plenty of old-timers mourn the passing of the neighbourhood they used to know.

Yet this international flavour is, mainly, exciting. It acts as a counterpoint to the anarchic character of young London's street life. Park and City has the parade of punks down the King's Road each Saturday; the art colleges in Soho; the pop music in a hundred pubs and clubs; the new and slightly crazy art galleries, which are increasingly positioning themselves to the east of the centre. Lots of Londoners sigh and tut-tut at all of this. They should be smiling. The quirkiness of London's youth culture – as we shall see later – is what makes Park and City the centre of what could be the world's most exciting twenty-first century city.

Brookstown
The second great region of London is a narrow strip of land that almost encircles Park and City. It stretches from Islington in the north-east, through Kentish Town and

Camden Town, Maida Vale and Queen's Park, then turns sharply south through Shepherd's Bush, Hammersmith and Fulham, crosses the river to Putney, Wandsworth, Clapham and Battersea, and reaches east to take in Herne Hill and Dulwich. Call it Brookstown, in honour of Roy Brooks, the estate agent whose tireless sale of houses within its borders helped to make it what it is.

What it is is upwardly mobile, or in Londonspeak "gentrified", meaning that within the last two decades it has been transformed from a working-class area to a middle-class one. This is not, of course, true of all of Brookstown. There are some areas – parts of Islington, the Irish enclave in Kilburn, the huge public housing estates around the White City stadium – that are as depressed as any part of London. But it is the area, above all, that has benefited from one of the most significant motors of British social change this century – the obsession with home ownership.

In 1910 only about 10% of dwellings in Britain were owned by the families who lived in them, the rest were rented from private landlords. By 1950 the position had changed, and by now it has changed dramatically. Only about 10% of dwellings are now privately rented. Brookstown is the area where you can see how the changing pattern of tenure changes districts. The novels of George Gissing set at the end of the nineteenth century, or of Antonia White, set before and after the First World War, are peopled with families who lived in relatively genteel circumstances (Mr Pooter, of *The Diary of a Nobody,* speaks for them all) but did not own their home. Contrast that with Brookstown now. The sons and daughters of Park and City have been moving there for 20 years, buying their houses from working-class home owners or small landlords.

Islington demonstrates the process of gentrification particularly acutely. Its attractive, mainly flat-fronted, houses were built in the late eighteenth and early nineteenth centuries, partly to service the demand for

white-collar labour in the City. But the area fell on hard
times, and by the 1950s was run-down and depressing, its
houses converted into shoddy flats. Many of them still
are, but the opening of the Victoria underground line in
1968 was the catalyst for an enormous change. The new
line made access from Islington to the West End much
easier, so prices started to go up. A new word,
"winkling", was coined for the practice of some
unscrupulous estate agents who persuaded – or "wink-
led" – the working-class owners of houses there to sell at
vast profits to the first wave of gentrifiers. Yet though the
elegant houses in Islington's nice squares have always
attracted young professionals – as have the similar,
though slightly less elegant, houses in Camden Town –
north Brookstown has never looked remotely like
Holland Park and Kensington, the western residential
areas of Park and City. Upper Street in Islington and
Camden High Street both look remarkably tatty, for all the
gentrified houses behind them and the increasing
numbers of upmarket shops that dot their facades. They
are worlds away from the ski-shop-to-fashion-store
parade that lines Kensington High Street.

In part, the continuing tattiness of these parts of
Brookstown is because it still has substantial public
housing estates. It has, too, many 80-year old developments owned by housing associations, who have been
playing a quasi-charitable role in London's housing for a
century. In part, the tattiness is because inner-north
London is the natural home of young first-timers in the
city – those who arrive with not much money, straight
from college, as often as not working in the public sector.
Upper Street had, until recently, two venues within a
hundred yards of each other that encapsulated these
newcomers' tastes: the excellent pub theatre at the King's
Head, and the no less excellent Hope & Anchor, venue
throughout the 1970s for the best of London's pub-rock.
Camden and Islington still feel as if they are the home of
fringe theatre, rock music (the Camden Palace, a huge

converted cinema in Mornington Crescent, is packed every night with London's young) and more recent showbiz fads like alternative cabaret.

Unsurprisingly, this collection of the young, public sector tenants, and those who first braved the now old-hat epithet "trendy" by making their homes in those flat-fronted houses, tend to be supporters of the political left. In particular, it is north Brookstown that has been the main ideological powerhouse of the "new" London Labour Party. "Socialist Republics", the right-wing press calls the councils of Islington and Camden, revelling in their sometimes strange grants to pressure groups. Yet the appeal of the Labour Party in these areas is no accident. Its strategy is closely identified in the public mind with Ken Livingstone, who became leader of the Greater London Council (GLC) in 1981 at 34, and led it with great verve until its abolition earlier this year. Livingstone is a master politician and self-publicist, in an age when to be the former you have to be the latter as well. I once claimed at a party that he was the best known Londoner ever – meaning that more Londoners would recognise him in a pub than would have recognised any of his predecessors – and no one present could gainsay me. His great political coup, after he and some colleagues had got rid of the "moderate" Labour leadership that won the 1981 GLC elections, was to put together a coalition of those whom conventional politics had left behind. He appealed deliberately to the young, to feminists, blacks, gays, artists, cyclists, and any other single-issue group he could find. So successful was he at setting up an alternative political power base, at a time when the Labour Party nationally was in disarray, that the Conservative government was forced to abolish the GLC to get rid of him. True, there were, as we shall see later, other reasons for ending the GLC, some of which ministers no doubt believed in, but doing down Mr Livingstone was certainly one of them. Not that we have seen the last of him; he will fight a safe Labour seat at the next general election.

West of Camden lies the home of one of the most important components of Mr Livingstone's menagerie. Kilburn is where London's Irish community has its centre. Not long ago, it was common to be solicited for funds for the Irish Republican Army (IRA) in its depressing but full pubs. Never mind that the Irish community appears at first sight to have little in common with the youngsters of Camden Town; both groups were convinced by Mr Livingstone – rightly, as it happens – that conventional politics had paid little attention to their problems. Both signed up enthusiastically with what they saw as a new Labour Party.

South-west of Kilburn, Brookstown swings through White City, an odd neighbourhood dominated by mammoth council estates mixed with an uneasy community of broadcasters, drawn there by the BBC television studios, and then down to Hammersmith. Hammersmith should be classic gentrification territory; King Street, its main shopping artery, is but a stone's throw from the end of Kensington High Street, and it provides a natural place for office development halfway between the West End and Heathrow. Yet despite quite grotesque price rises for cottages (£18,000 five years ago; £80,000 now) in what estate agents winsomely call "Brackenbury Village" the area as a whole has never quite made it. King's Mall shopping centre, despite its Safeway supermarket and Habitat, always appears to have rather too many empty shops for comfort. The reason for edginess in Hammersmith is almost entirely because of political squabbling. A huge island-site at Hammersmith Broadway, above the tube station, has been virtually derelict for 15 years. Local politicians have continued to disagree over whether to devote it to offices (which is what those King Street shops need to provide more custom) or homes. Round the corner, the theatre and art centre at the Riverside Studios have similarly had to put up with a decade of uncertainty as councillors try to decide whether they do or don't want one of London's liveliest cultural venues on their doorstep.

Further south still, in Fulham, the gentrification of rows of three-bedroomed terraced houses is now almost complete, with the fashionable shops of the King's Road snaking ever westward and the flats and pubs full of Sloane Rangers, the extravagant and sometimes idle children of the rich. Putney, across the river, has gone upmarket too. Both these districts were recently solid Labour parliamentary seats; in the 1983 general election they were both won by the Conservatives. Brookstown then swings east again, to today's hottest area of gentrification – the corridor along the south bank that takes in Wandsworth, Battersea and Clapham. This was slower to get the house converters, probably because most of it depends for transport to Park and City on buses and British Rail trains, not the tube. But many of the houses here offer what Camden, Fulham and Putney cannot – real gardens – and they are taking on a suburban air as well as the trendiness of north Brookstown. Dulwich, centred on its nineteenth-century college, at the eastern edge of this crescent, has always had the aspect of a suburban village – remarkably so for somewhere so close to central London. Appropriately, it is the area that the Prime Minister, Mrs Margaret Thatcher, has decided to retire to. She has bought a £400,000 home backing on to a Dulwich golf course. This is exactly the right location for someone who wants the impression of suburban space while continuing to be obsessed with the cut and thrust of urban public life. That mixture of as gracious living as you can afford behind front doors, coupled with a mad rush for the earning-holes of Park and City once you open them, is the essence of Brookstown.

Crescent

While Brookstown snakes round Park and City to the west, to the east the third of London's regions mocks it like a distorted mirror. Crescent stretches from Finsbury Park and Tottenham in the north, through Stoke Newington, Dalston and Hackney, into the old East End of Stepney and Bow, crosses the river to Bermondsey and then curves westwards to Peckham, Brixton and Lambeth. This area, remember, is contiguous to some of the world's most expensive real estate, occupied by some of its most highly paid professionals. You wouldn't know it to walk around most of Crescent. Seven Sisters Road in Finsbury Park is a traditional, and dingy, red-light area. Tottenham's Broadwater Farm Estate was the scene of a vicious riot in 1985 when guns were trained on the police and a constable was stabbed to death. Stoke Newington has poor black and Jewish communities, both dogged by racial attacks; Haggerston and Dalston, just to the south, have been strongholds of fascist thugs for years.

Much of the old East End is a depressing jumble of high-rise flats, put there by ineffective and sometimes corrupt local government, slum clearance, with nothing put in its place, and unemployment – eight of Crescent's parliamentary constituencies have unemployment rates above 20%. The docks that gave the East End, north of the river, its economic life are all closed. So are the Surrey Docks to the south. In 20 years, 20,000 jobs have been lost in the upstream docks; London's port is now 17 miles away, at Tilbury. Deptford is known to the rest of the country mainly because of a fire in 1981 that killed 13 black youngsters at a party, in circumstances never fully explained. Peckham has council estates peculiar for their squalor and vandalism even by London's standards. Brixton – "ah! Brixton" say the know-alls – is notorious for having spawned riots against the police in both 1981 and 1985.

There is no point in denying that Crescent has plenty of squalor, and substantial poverty too. It makes up one of Britain's largest areas of multiple social deprivation. Equally, there is no point in pretending that the whole of the area is run-down. Canonbury and the beautiful squares in de Beauvoir Town have been rescued from dereliction; Stoke Newington has Brookstown-like streets; so does Hackney, especially round Victoria Park. Dockland, north and south of the Thames, represents the largest scheme of urban renewal in Europe, complete with a planned airport and a projected 10 billion square foot financial services complex at Canary Wharf. Old gems of industrial architecture like St Katharine's Dock are already tourist attractions; gentrified housing, some of it in converted nineteenth-century warehouses, is increasingly available north and south of the river. Shoreditch, Bethnal Green and Whitechapel are being revitalised through the chaotic business drive of the Bengali rag-trade. Brixton, the siren song of the gloomsters, has always had pockets of spectacular early nineteenth-century housing that have never been allowed to decay; bordering areas like Stockwell and Kennington have proved increasingly popular with those who like big houses a stone's throw from Westminster.

What happens to Crescent in the future depends more distinctly than most commentators like to admit on race relations. This is the area where, traditionally, foreign immigrants to London have settled – Jews in Shoreditch and Stoke Newington, Huguenots in Bethnal Green, Chinese in Limehouse. More recently, Bengalis and East African Asians have settled in the East End and West Indians in Brixton and Lambeth. About 50% of Shoreditch and Whitechapel is now Asian, and the same proportion of central Brixton is black. London has been good news for most of these groups. The Jewish communities in the northern and eastern suburbs escaped from the East End earlier this century; the Huguenots long before that. East African Asians already look like following them, and the Bengali community around Whitechapel certainly shows enough verve to find its own pot of gold.

The really important question is whether the black community in Brixton can manage the same upwardly mobile path. There has been little sign of it so far. Most of those earlier groups were discriminated against in the employment market, but none more than blacks have been in the past 30 years; blacks are 60%–100% more likely to be unemployed than equally qualified whites. Moreover, those earlier immigrants had something which the West Indians who came to Britain in the 1950s did not. They had an indigenous entrepreneurial culture that enabled them to set up economic life when avenues to conventional success were closed to them. What the black community has, by contrast, is a sense of energy and style that at its best can transform an area into one long party, but at its worst can react to unemployment and racial harassment with the frightening consequences seen in the riots of 1981 and 1985.

Here again, the politics of London's Labour Party throughout the 1980s take on a critical role. Ken Livingstone says, proudly, that the one achievement that no future historian of London will be able to take away from his time at the GLC is the extent to which he has put the position of London's black and Asian community on the map. He is right. Something like 16% of London's population is now black or Asian, and it is in Crescent that the scale, opportunities and problems of this change in London's character can be seen most clearly. This is the area where blacks and Asians have become most heavily politicised; most of the leaders of the campaign for "black sections" in the national Labour Party are Crescent politicians like Diane Abbott, who is almost certain to be the first black woman member of parliament. Though a West Indian doctor, Lord Pitt, was the chairman of the Greater London Council during a Labour administration 15 years ago, Mr Livingstone can fairly say that his Labour predecessors did not place a high priority on the problems of black and Asian people in Crescent. For too many Conservative politicians, those people are still regarded as "immigrants", despite the fact that most black and brown Londoners are now London-born as well as London-bred.

It will need more than the raising of white Londoners' consciousness about their black neighbours to transform the worst areas of Crescent. It will need more, too, than government-sponsored development corporations like the one which has been so successful in dockland – indeed, if public money was the answer to the problems of Crescent, they would have been solved long ago. The path away from economic decay in this inner-city area will only be taken if the black community wants to take it, and has the confidence to take it. Some small signs suggest that change may be in the air. Some senior policemen, for example, say that the 1981 riots were a watershed for the Metropolitan Police. The force has never been good at recruiting black policemen, and this led to an absence of sensitivity in its handling of the black community – and that is putting it in the mildest terms possible. After the publication of Lord Scarman's report on the 1981 riots, the police realised that they had to put their house in order. There were too many racists in the force, and too few officers who understood the needs of blacks for good, but not heavy-handed, policing. These same officers say that the 1985 riots brought about a similar change in the black community. The death of Constable Blakelock at Broadwater Farm, they argue, has convinced the great mass of law-abiding blacks that they must accept responsibility for channelling the energy of their youngsters into productive rather than destructive ends. Take that, perhaps, with a pinch of salt – Scotland Yard's record of knowing what makes London's black community tick has not been so great that too much weight should be placed on its latest predictions.

Less easy to dismiss are two other developments in Crescent – the growth and health of black churches, and the demand by black parents for good schools for their children. Some black parents, indeed, have gone so far as to remove their children from state schools, which they think under-educate their children with lots of trendy ideas, and place them in private schools where they will get a traditional British education. Both movements, it can be plausibly argued, attest to a black community taking its future into its own hands, and out of a London whose values have done little for the future of the children of its most recent, and most lively, ethnic community.

Micawber

Why call south London Micawber? Because something terrific is always about to turn up, or so, at least, say those who live there, south London patriots all. Those who live in west or north London, by contrast, would say that you would have to be jingoistically attached to south London to tolerate it. Well . . . let us not take sides. Some of south London counts among London's most undervalued assets; other parts are duller than it is polite to say.

Micawber stretches from the parkland of Wimbledon in the east – true London village country this, with a view from the All England Lawn Tennis Club up the hill that is almost worthy of a Constable landscape. But in typical Micawber style, the promise is not fulfilled. South of Wimbledon are the boring flatlands of Raynes Park, Merton and Morden, crammed, so it always seems, with do-it-yourself shops and did-it-themselves, tasteless conversions of Edwardian terraces. Then, to the east, starts what Steve Grant of *Time Out* magazine wistfully refers to as south London's "golden triangle"; the Streatham-Balham-Tooting township, small nineteenth-century farming villages transformed by the railways into crammed dormitory townships for Park and City.

It certainly looked golden to me when, as a 15-year old, newly hitch-hiked to the smoke from the north to stay with a friend's sister (a teacher; somehow, the golden triangle attracts teachers) I was amazed to discover that Streatham, a place I had never heard of, had more entertainment and shops in one section of its High Street than the whole of my sizeable home town. My friend and I were not allowed into the flash Mecca dance hall – no ties – an event I have ever since considered to be quintessentially south London.

Flash, Micawber has remained. Though the popular television series *Minder* is in fact filmed in Fulham and Hammersmith, its milieu of ever-so-slightly crooked car dealers on the make epitomises south London. Streatham, one always feels, is the place to go for cheap watches sold in the back bar of a pub by someone just back from an autumn break in Ibiza, with a parked Ford Escort XR3i outside.

The flash harries do not have all the golden triangle to themselves, though. Balham and Tooting are both being gentrified; Balham, especially, is closer to the office jobs in Park and City than most people recognised until very recently. The houses are spacious, cheaper than in Brookstown, and there are also, or so locals will tell you, plenty of parks, though critics from north or west London are on safer ground than usual in finding both Tooting and Streatham Commons dull slabs of open space. West of Streatham the land gets hillier again, until you reach the radio mast at Crystal Palace, just above the National Sports Centre (an example of a facility of which London has far too few). Sydenham, Honor Oak, Catford and Hither Green all appear, at least to a Brookstowner like myself, to be full of terraces perched crazily up the side of hills, the like of which are unknown in much of west London.

Beyond these areas – all quite densely populated – come two of London's towns-within-a-city, Beckenham and Bromley. Bromley, in particular, hardly feels part of the metropolis. It was entirely predictable that the legal action which scuppered Mr Livingstone's cheap fares policy for London's tubes and buses in 1981 was started by the Conservative councillors who run this borough. Its shopping centre would not disgrace cities twice the size in the north or Midlands of England, and it feels big enough to have suburbs of its own. Lots of 1930s bungalows (uncommon in most of outlying London) and some very ritzy houses are dotted among stands of tall pine trees. This is bank manager and senior civil servant territory, a decent British Rail commute to Park and City and close enough to the M25 orbital motorway to get out of town, to Kent, Surrey or the continent. Maybe, just, something really has turned up in Bromley. It may not have character but it does have a certain sense of its worth as an independent town, not dependent on the rest of London for its wellbeing.

2
MORE A COUNTRY THAN A CITY: OUTER LONDON

Downland

For real self-sufficiency you have to get right out of inner London. Try Croydon, the capital of Downland, an area that sprawls for some 20 miles along London's southern boundary. Croydon is Britain's twelfth largest city, just larger than Coventry, with whom it shares a peculiarly American aspect. Those modern tower blocks full of offices are not as large as the ones in any self-respecting American city, of course, but the Whitgift shopping centre next to them, and the urban motorways that take traffic through the town, all help to make the place look as much like Birmingham, Alabama as Birmingham, England.

These developments are deliberate; they followed a decision by the local council to turn this suburb into a major office and retailing centre in the early 1960s. And that means that the bustle of Croydon's shops and offices is untypical of Downland. This, above all, is where the rich suburban life of the Kent and Surrey stockbroker belts touches the noise and occasional squalor of the metropolis. The two cultures can be seen clearly within a mile or two of Croydon; compare Purley, a southern extension of the flash harry golden triangle, immortalised a decade ago by Monty Python ("*Purley*; say no more, nudge-nudge, wink-wink"), with Chipstead, a stockbrokers' village on the edge of the downs so perfect and well kept that it always feels fake.

To the south west of Croydon the same betwixt and between feel can be detected in Sutton, Ewell and Epsom.

But as one moves past Epsom Downs, site of the world's most famous horse-race, the Derby, for more than 200 years, you hit the Surrey Downs, full of beeches and pines. Surrey County Council has a remarkable 40-year-old record of preserving the beauty of its north-eastern corner. You can drive from Heathrow airport along the M25 to the junction with the M23 (which leads down to Gatwick airport) and see precious few houses, let alone factories. What seem to be toy farms and houses nestle in the folds of the downs. Beyond the motorway, towns like Leatherhead and Dorking provide some of Britain's most comfortable living.

The thing that threatens this quiet peace is, of course, the M25 itself, the 121-mile long motorway that circles London and which will be completed this year. The barbarians are just inside its ring, and as industry finds everything in central London progressively more crowded it will seek to move out to the fringes of the motorway. The Surrey section is already proving particularly attractive, because it is the part that links the two large airports. Surrey County Council has let it be known that it is determined to preserve its hills for recreation and – let it be said – for their rich inhabitants. If the matter was left to the Prime Minister and market forces they would not succeed; but folks have been saying that this remarkably unspoilt corner of southern England would be bricked over for years, and have been proved wrong. Don't bet against Surrey's local politicos keeping industry out again.

Pressure on land for industrial use is less acute in the eastern, Kentish sector of Downland. Though closer to the channel ports, this area is less well situated for Heathrow and for the corridor of high-tech industries that stretches from London to Bristol. Without ever quite achieving the lustrous look of the Surrey quadrant of Downland, the hills and walks round the old Kentish airfields of Biggin Hill and Farnborough are pretty enough, their Kentish villages ever so slightly less genteel than those in Surrey.

Further east still is the quite magnificent Darenth valley, famous for the mystical nineteenth-century landscape painting of Samuel Palmer, leading up to Farningham (where you can see one of the many village duckponds that dot Downland). At least, it was magnificent. It has been spoilt (though not ruined) by a spur of the M25 reaching up to the river crossing at Dartford. Just inside the motorway, small towns like Chislehurst, and suburban territory like Orpington, remind you that you still belong to London. If not quite Micawber, by Orpington you no longer have the feel that the *leitmotif* of your community is a stockbroker in the village pub at Sunday lunchtime, large gin-and-tonic in hand. The pub will not be so quaint; the drink may be beer, and the job will be less well paid than the broker's.

Northern Heights

Why don't London's northern suburbs feel like the heart of Downland? There is far less up there of the fake attempt to countrify the fringes of a city, far less rejection, conscious or otherwise, of the urban. Northern Heights, the sixth of London's distinct regions, stretches in a wedge from Tottenham, Hornsey and Hampstead in the south, northwards through Finchley, Barnet, Mill Hill, Totteridge and Enfield to the Hertfordshire suburbs. Its south-eastern corner can be very seedy indeed – this is, after all, close to the inner city, and streets like Tottenham High Road and Hornsey Lane are as depressing as any in the heart of Crescent. To their west, Highgate and Hampstead would be regarded by some as northern extensions of Brookstown. But both of them are old genteel areas; the impact of gentrification has been felt less there than in Islington or Camden, largely because they never fell into disrepair in the way that Brookstown did.

   This is particularly true of Hampstead, which, says Simon Jenkins, chronicler of London's buildings and villages, "has always been a suburb and no one fastidious about that term should pretend otherwise". Proof, were any needed, might be in Hampstead's role for nearly 300 years as a health resort for those who wanted to escape London's noisome air. Hampstead is high, (its tube station, inhabitants never tire of telling the unwary, is the deepest in London). Views to the south from the top of Hampstead Heath, up by Jack Straw's Castle pub or the Spaniards Inn, stretch right to the South Downs. Similar views are to be had as one moves east from Hampstead, through Highgate (always less attractive than it promises to be) to Muswell Hill, and thence by footpath to Alexandra Palace.

It is from here, more than anywhere else in London, that one can see the extent to which the City – six miles to the south – has driven so much of the capital's recent economic development. West of the City the few high-rise buildings – the Shell Centre, Millbank Tower, the Hilton Hotel – stick out incongruously in a townscape that has remained remarkably low-rise. But the City is rapidly becoming a riot of new buildings; the new Stock Exchange building, Richard Rogers' Crystal-Palace-in-the-sky for the Lloyd's insurance market, and the NatWest tower are beginning to form a homogeneous and curiously exciting whole. Even the three-towered Barbican Centre, which the closer you get to it looks more and more like a fly-blown wasteland, can look dramatic from Alexandra Park.

To the north of Hampstead is its Garden Suburb, a collection of quiet streets of fine early twentieth-century houses. Then comes Golders Green, still a village until the 1920s, but turned into a thriving suburb with the arrival of the tube, and Finchley, whose two parts, Finchley Central and East Finchley, lie either side of the North Circular Road. This is where the Jewish community moved when it left the East End between the wars; and it is where Jewish refugees from central Europe settled at the same time. It is not a Jewish community of the size or cohesion of those that would be found in some parts of the United States of America. Mrs Thatcher's parliamentary constituency in Finchley is often said to have the largest Jewish vote of any of Britain's 650 seats, yet it would be surprising in the extreme if that vote amounted to more than 20% of the electorate.

Yet the Jewish influence is out of all proportion to its population. One measure of that is the extent to which London's Jewish community has provided the ballast of Mrs Thatcher's government since 1979. Her Chancellor of the Exchequer, Nigel Lawson, her ex-Trade and Industry secretary, Leon Brittan, and her ideologist, Sir Keith Joseph, are all Jewish. So are two brothers who are Mrs Thatcher's creations, Lord (David) Young, her Employment secretary, and Stuart Young, the Chairman of the board of governors of the BBC. Others of the same community close to her include the Wolfson family of Great Universal Stores, and Sir Basil Feldman, at one time Chairman of the Conservatives' national committee.

There is no mystery about the Prime Minister's personal preference for London's Jews. Despite her small-town origins, she is very much an urban person; the country bores her. She admires Jewish drive (Lord Young, she has said, never brings her problems, only solutions). Besides, the Jewish community, according to some observers, looks after her Finchley seat. What is slightly surprising is the preference of the Jewish community for the Conservative party. Earlier in the century, the experience of Jewish refugees from eastern Europe or Germany tended to make the community socialist in its outlook. Arnold Wesker's trilogy of plays following the fortunes of the Jewish East End Kahn family left no doubt that such events as the battle of Cable Street, when East Enders fought Oswald Mosley's fascists in the 1930s, were an important part of the British Jewish experience. But that kind of East End community spirit is no more; and that kind of Jewishness appears to have died with it.

What did not die was the Jewish sense of civilised

discourse and intellectualism. Hampstead and its environs are the only part of London where one feels that musical evenings are an unforced, natural part of the order of things. Its bookshops are full and its restaurants, pubs and cake-shops (there is a good one just at the edge of the Heath) always look as if their conversation is more lively and intelligent than that in the rest of London.

All this could be wishful thinking but Hampstead does have an indefinable mood about it, not ruined by trendiness, which makes it one of London's most pleasant places. And something of that pleasantness infects the suburbs across the North Circular Road. Totteridge Lane is worth looking at; a strip of millionaire's houses forever, I always think, full of ponies. Arkley, a little further north, is the closest that Northern Heights gets to the *ersatz* villages of Downland. Mill Hill is real suburbia, Barnet even more so, and thence beyond, into the Hertfordshire countryside, on the road, so signs always used to say, to "Hatfield and the North". (A Northerner, I always thought those signs spoke worlds about the relative importance that Londoners attached to their suburbs and the rest of the country). Though by no means unpleasant, the countryside here is less lush than that of Downland, its villages, though some very rich indeed (try Northaw, home of Cecil Parkinson, another of Mrs Thatcher's favourites), less perfectly preserved than those in the south.

Waterside
With the exception of dockland, there is only one area of London where the River Thames is a constant presence. This is another wedge, running from Hammersmith Bridge south-west, and taking in Barnes, Kew, Chiswick, Richmond, Twickenham, Teddington, Kingston and Hampton before it rolls into the Surrey golfing suburbs of Virginia Water, Weybridge and Sunningdale. Call it Waterside – not Riverside, for one of the features of this

region is the number of ponds and gravel pits towards its western boundaries that are now almost as much a source of recreation as the river itself.

This is largely flat country, which makes the views from such hills as do exist seem more dramatic than you would expect. The most famous is from the terraces on Richmond Hill, looking along the river to Twickenham, Petersham and Ham – a prospect that can hardly have altered in 200 years. A very different view, looking into London rather than away from it, can be obtained from the RAF war memorial at Runnymede, worth a visit if only because it is a peaceful example of the wonders that the Commonwealth War Graves Commission can work. Set high above the river, the terrace of the monument looks out over the whole of south-west London, with a haze of the city centre visible on the skyline. To its north, around Royal Holloway College's pile of Victorian Gothic, (as good as Gilbert Scott's St Pancras Station, for those who like that kind of thing), starts the belt of sandy heathland that stretches from London through Hampshire and Dorset to the south coast. This is a curious landscape, not quite what one expects from southern England, with pines dotted on scrubby hills almost, on a summer's day, like California or Provence.

This is outer Waterside. Its inner edges could only be England, and only in that part of England – London – where merchants have always been able to escape just a few miles from their place of work to homes of remarkable comfort and quiet. You can walk or, better, bicycle, along the southern bank of the river from Hammersmith to Kingston and for much of the way find it impossible to believe that you are in the middle of a city. The playing fields of St Paul's School – *the* boys' public school these days – lead to the village of Barnes, with its partially burnt-out parish church, duckpond and small art galleries. Opposite, on the northern shore, Chiswick Mall leads to what little remains of Chiswick village (cut in half by the six-lane Great West Road) and thence to some elegant early nineteenth-century houses in Gunnersbury, and the lovely terrace on the water's edge at Strand-on-the-Green. Still staying on the northern shore, the next stop is Kew Green (where the pub once stayed open all day, and was populated by a raffish crowd of doctors and second-hand car salesmen, only some of whom had come for what must have been one of London's first designer contraceptive machines), and then Kew Gardens.

The gardens are an acquired taste; some people find the land too flat, the greenhouses overpowering, and, above all, the constant roar of jets starting their descent to Heathrow disconcerting. But they can be terribly romantic; I once spent a tearful day walking through them with my girlfriend before flying off to a job in Chicago. (This story has a happy ending; I flew back on one of those 'planes a year later, and married her). Richmond, too, has its fans, of which I confess I have never been one. The town centre has a disappointing collection of suburban shops. The green, to be found down a passage crammed with antique shops, always looks too perfect and too – well – rich. The pubs are nothing to write home about, save for those who want to capture a bit of rock music history, for it was in Richmond pubs that some of the Rolling Stones' first gigs were held. (This part of Waterside is a must for rock historians; Eel Pie Island, just down the Thames, was once run as a musicians' collective, and later owned by The Who's Pete Townshend). The 2,000 acres of Richmond Park, untouched in some senses since Norman times, leave me cold. While others rave about the herds of deer mooching about, I remember that they mean that the coppices have to be neatly fenced in. This is artificial countryside; Hampstead Heath is much more like the real thing.

But for those who like English country houses, the next five miles of river downstream from Richmond are a must. You can catch Marble Hill House, Ham, Strawberry Hill, and thence to Hampton Court Palace, surrounded by the flatness of Bushy Park (more deer), or, a little to the north of Richmond through old Isleworth, Robert Adam's exquisite Syon House. The towns along this stretch of river are not as interesting as they should be; Twickenham is dull, Teddington only a little better, Kingston, though well situated on the river, a testament to how not to plan roads. But tucked away are some nice collections of Edwardian houses – try those, for example, behind Strawberry Hill Station – and a remarkable collection of good pubs, much better than those in Richmond. Waterside is the place in London where 1950s-style pub-going (men in handlebar moustaches drinking pints of Young's or Fuller's, talking of cars and girls) seems still to be in vogue. Indeed, for the perfect example of what London life was like 20 years ago, you could not do better than to spend a Saturday on an excursion to one of the area's two racecourses, Kempton and Sandown Parks. (The April day of the Whitbread Gold Cup and the Guardian Derby Trial at Sandown is a good one). You could take in Hampton Court Palace on your way and drink down your profits afterwards at somewhere like The Swan on the river at Twickenham. It's not the multi-racial, edgy, yet exciting, London of much of today's inner city, but there's no doubt that Waterside has its charm.

Heathrow
North of Waterside lies another wedge leading west-wards, this one totally dominated by London's main airport at Heathrow. Dominated in two senses, first, because the main flight path to the airport follows the M4 motorway westwards from central London, so that by Hammersmith or Kew the 'planes are an ever-present feature; second, because since it was first used in 1939 (it was opened as a civil airport in 1946, taking over from the Croydon aerodrome, which is still visible just off the Purley Way) it has been the economic motor for much of

west London. Heathrow now generates, directly or indirectly, some 70,000 jobs.

And it's a mess. Those used to airports built on green field sites like Charles de Gaulle, Paris, or O'Hare, Chicago, will despair when first they turn off the motorway, and, after a short drive through a tunnel (short if you're lucky – logjammed if you're not), hit the baffling above-ground rabbit warren of Heathrow's central three terminals. Even New York's JFK looks good compared to this. Indefatigable as ever, Simon Jenkins reckons that all three terminals are worth a second look; this must be to check that they really are as awful as they first seem, and indeed they are. Terminal 3 on a busy Saturday – say, just before Christmas – is my idea of hell. I once saw a man die from a heart attack at a queue in the check-in counter and I wasn't at all surprised.

Of course, it's not hard to find reasons, even excuses, for the mess. Heathrow, as advertisements never tire of telling all those still prepared to listen, is the world's busiest international airport. Its 30m passengers a year (growing, growing) make it the world's largest airport outside the USA. Indeed, it is a mistake to think of Heathrow as a piece of England, or London, at all. It really acts as the gateway to Europe for the rest of the world. In 1984 Heathrow had 25m international passengers. Frankfurt, second in Europe for international passengers, had just 13m. (Gatwick, London's second airport, is the third biggest international airport in Europe). All this is going to get bigger. A fourth terminal, mercifully removed from the three central ones, opened in 1986, and a recent public inquiry hinted very strongly indeed that the 1990s might see a fifth, on the site of a sewage works at the western edge of the present perimeter.

The international visitor will say, why wasn't it planned better? Why does everything take so long? Why is it so cramped? And the answer, surprisingly, is that Heathrow is a mess because of something of which Britain can be proud – the extent to which its system of town and country planning, has, since 1947, allowed those members of the public most affected by major development projects to participate in decision-making. Only the most starry-eyed environmentalist would claim that the delays thus caused (London's airports have been a bone of contention for 25 years) are always justified, but in turn, only those most aggressively determined to give developers all that they want would deny that the public inquiry system has preserved some communities from more horrors than they deserve. The shambles at Heathrow, you can plausibly argue, is the price you pay for the fact that Britain still does some things in a tolerably democratic way. Ask the French whether the speed with which their major projects are pushed through always makes for happiness.

South and east of Heathrow, with the exception of Southall, is mainly depressing: inter-war housing huddling together for protection from the jets. There are, however, a few fine churches in what were once prosperous Middlesex villages and Osterley Park, with its largely Robert Adam house (clearly visible from the flightpath, from which you can also see how the M4 neatly dissected the great park). But Southall is different. The borough of Ealing (which takes in a large chunk of what we call Heathrow) has an estimated 26% of its population living in households whose head was born in the New Commonwealth or Pakistan, and most of it is in Southall. It is one of two areas of London (Whitechapel/ Spitalfields is the other) that those originally from the Indian sub-continent have made their own, and it is beginning to bristle with the unique entrepreneurialism of India.

This is not just a question of cinemas and restaurants. Increasingly, Southall's Indians are beginning to assert themselves and carve out an economy of their own away from the racism they met when they first settled there. Though mention of the word "riots" in London always conjures up Brixton, the most remarkable recent outbreak of urban unrest was in fact in Southall in 1981, when local Indian youths, tired of being pushed around by racist skinheads bussed in from the East End, burned down the pub where the thugs congregated. It was an affirmation of confidence that took most of the rest of London, and, one suspects, some of the older members of the Indian community as well, completely by surprise. West Indians were supposed to behave like that; Indians weren't. One side effect, according to some reports, is that Southall now has a number of gangs – all Indian – who fight for territory. Another has been the determination of the local community to get the Labour Party to select an Indian as a parliamentary candidate, with much accusations of meeting-packing from the old order. There will, no doubt, be other problems along the way before the Indian community plays its full part in London life. But it will happen, and the sheer energy of Southall proves that it will.

Economic energy of a different kind can be seen along the A30 and Great West Road. Their margins are dotted with 1930s factories, some of them extremely fine (though the Firestone factory, the finest of all, was torn down in 1980 when it looked as if it might be protected from redevelopment). These are testimony to the years between the wars when London, and especially west London, was Britain's boom region. Some estimates reckon that 80% of new factory building in Britain in the 1920s and 1930s came to London, and the surrounds of Heathrow is where you can see what it looks like. Catch, particularly, the Hoover building on the A40, which marks the boundary between the region of Heathrow and that of Metroland. Now immortalised in a song by Elvis Costello, it is an entirely unexpected Odeon-arch-architecture extravaganza, looking for all the world like a Hollywood studio.

Closer in to town, the somewhat uninteresting suburbs of Ealing and Acton stretch towards western Brookstown. Ealing bristles with family respectability; both John

Gummer, youthful ex-chairman of the Conservative Party, and Neil Kinnock, leader of the Labour Party, live there, together with their pretty wives and kids. It is Marks & Spencer two-piece-suit territory, the kind of place where young middle managers from the north settle with their families. But further in still is a real London gem, the Norman Shaw-designed late Victorian village of Bedford Park, with its houses so obviously influenced by William Morris and the Arts and Crafts Movement. Bedford Park has had plenty of satirists of its slightly prissy, self-consciously arty airs. Don't be fooled by the know-alls; it is very nice indeed, probably the area closest to the centre of London where you have the space – in your houses, gardens and streets – of a true suburb.

Metroland

It was the Metropolitan Railway Company, the first enterprise to lay down permanent way in the network that now makes up London Regional Transport's train services, that christened north-west London Metroland. Sir John Betjeman's celebration of it came much later (he made a memorable television programme on the region in the early 1970s), and Julian Barnes' evocative novel of the same name, describing what it was like growing up in London's suburbs, later still. The company's first line linked Hammersmith with the City; parts of it are remarkably similar to the elevated railways that New Yorkers or Chicagoans will be familiar with. But the railway that gave its name to London's eighth region stretched from Baker Street out into the Chiltern Hills. You can still travel by the Metropolitan line to Amersham, a typical market town in the Chilterns, and could once take the train almost to the suburbs of Oxford. True Metroland starts much closer to the city centre than that.

Indeed, this sector of London is by no means all leafy suburbia. Brent, the borough that links the suburbs with the city, has the highest proportion (33%) of black or Asian population of any London borough, together with the Irish community that we have already looked at in Kilburn. Brent's politics, almost inevitably, have always been troublesome, as the suburban Conservative wards towards the borough's northern edge are almost exactly matched by its Labour-voting Irish and black neighbourhoods. Some of London's most successful black politicians, like Russell Profitt, who will fight Lewisham for Labour at the next general election, have their bases in Brent. Paul Boateng, the black Chairman of the GLC's police committee, will fight one of Brent's seats for Labour. Ken Livingstone will fight another. He traded on his high reputation with both the black and Irish communities to secure the nomination over Reg Freeson, the Jewish sitting member. But not all of Brent's black population is enamoured with Labour. More than any other London borough, it has been the place for black parents' complaints that modern educational practices have not pushed their children to the limits of their ability. One black Labour councillor joined the Conservatives over the issue in a very public row; those left behind are now much more sensitive to the needs of parents than they once were, with a consequent growth of tension between some elements in the London Labour Party and their traditional supporters among the teachers' unions.

This south-eastern corner of Metroland was heavily industrialised from the time of the First World War. Park Royal, an industrial estate that lies between the A40 to Oxford and the North Circular Road, was first developed for munitions factories. Then food-processing and heavy industry followed, making it one of London's largest concentration of manufacturing industry. In common with the rest of Britain, these businesses have shed jobs over the last 20 years, which means that west London, always considered to be more prosperous than the east, has not escaped the ravages of the changing British economy.

Brent's unemployment rate is higher than the London average, and it has less of the tourist amenities or facilities for new service industries that can rescue some parts of the inner city. But it does have Brent Cross, at the junction of the North Circular and the M1 motorway to the north, London's first out-of-town shopping mall. This is all right for those who like such things but without any of the really mind-blowing extravagance of the best American examples. And Brent has one of the monuments in London that most Britons from outside the capital recognise immediately; Wembley Stadium, built in time for the 1923 football Cup Final, whose twin towers dominate the view from both the North Circular Road and the main railway line from London to Birmingham. The glamour of Wembley is best captured on television. In reality, it is tired, patched up, and tawdry. Still, you can have fun there, of a rather cruel kind. I like the greyhound racing on a winter's evening, when you can sit behind glass, eat a tolerable meal, and have waitresses collect your bets from your table while the poor dogs (and some poor punters) huddle for protection from the elements outside your window.

Wembley Park, beyond the stadium, is one of the mock "Tudorbethan" estates that followed the railway. There are plenty of others, like Moor Park, Croxley Green and Pinner, but with the exception of some of the earlier developments, which managed to keep space round the houses constructed in the first half of this century, I have never found the elixir that makes students of British vernacular architecture so keen on the area. Harrow has its fans. It has a nice hilly situation and a famous public school; indeed, for many years it was the second public school (after Eton) in the country. But it seems less in the news these days. No recent old boy has approached the eminence of Winston Churchill, though this may be because Harrovians are less inclined than Etonians to rule and more inclined to make money. Whatever the reason, its confines, and the village that surrounds it, provide a convenient stopping point on the way out of London to the Chilterns, which really are worth discovering – deep wooded valleys, cosy pubs and curious flint-speckled stone-built houses – but still largely ignored by the millions who live on their doorstep.

New Bow Bells

A true cockney, it was always said, was one who was born within the sound of the Bow Bells, in the East End. Not now; insofar as any remnant of the old working-class London still exists, it is not to be found in the East End – now the place for tourists, dereliction, the glossiness of the dockland rebirth, and Bengalis – but further east and south. New Bow Bells, the last of our regions of London, stretches from Epping Forest in the north, round in an arc through Romford, Ilford and Dagenham, and then south of the river to take in Erith, Crayford, and Welling. Closer in to the centre, it includes the "semi-detached" East End – Plaistow, Leytonstone and West Ham – and the contrasting south-London areas of Charlton, Woolwich and Blackheath. Thamesmead, London's own new town, is prime New Bow Bells country; most of its first inhabitants were from the old East End.

There may be a social unity to this area, but there is no geographical one – or at least, not yet. There is no river crossing between the Blackwall Tunnel from the Isle of Dogs to the Greenwich peninsula, and the Dartford Tunnel, which carries the M25 under the Thames 15 miles further east (though there is a free ferry at Woolwich). The new east London river crossing (known as Elric), projected to go from Beckton, at the easternmost end of dockland, to Thamesmead, will do more than lock the new developments at dockland into the national road network. It will also unite the two, unequal, halves of a distinct region.

East London is big. There is no one place from which you can see just how big it is, though the view east from the newly opened catwalk above Tower Bridge gives some idea of its size – and its flatness. Only the ridge from Blackheath along Shooter's Hill really breaks the monotony. To the north, the suburbs of Chingford and Woodford are mostly uninteresting. Woodford was Winston Churchill's constituency; Chingford is that of the Conservative Party Chairman, Norman Tebbit, and I've often thought that the stream of right-wing, nationalist populism in both those politicians catches perfectly the world view of east Londoners who have made it, and escaped to the suburbs. Further out, Epping Forest is still largely unspoilt (the M25 is tunnelled under part of it) and still acts as something of a lung for East Londoners – though most of them, by now, would be more familiar with the air on the beach at Torremolinos than they would with the leafy dells of the forest. Ilford and Romford – cabdrivers' country – stretch out towards Essex, the most mysterious (and second most populous) of all English counties to outsiders, perched at the edge of the island, its brackish creeks and inlets leading to nowhere but the great sky above the North Sea. This is where you will discover real east London overspill, in Brentwood, Billericay, and the well-run, socialist-controlled new town of Basildon ("Moscow-on-the-Thames" government ministers sometimes call it). Eventually you reach the sea at the down-market resort of Southend, famous for the lines of coaches that used to dump thousands of East Enders by the seaside on bank holidays, some of the first Mods and Rockers fights of the early 1960s, and, later, its own brand of gutsy pub-rock (Alison Moyet is from Basildon, and sounds just like you would expect).

Coming back into London along the A13, you pass first through Grays and Thurrock and then hit Dagenham. As Park Royal was to west London, so Dagenham was to the east. The Ford factory started producing cars in 1931, and with the exception of the now-privatised British Telecom, remains the largest private-sector employer in

the city, though its 16,000-plus workers are dwarfed by
those who work in public administration. Other industry
followed Ford, giving Dagenham a degree of prosperity
that it has never lost, however precarious the future of
mass motor-car production in Britain might be. Continuing west, across Barking Flats and past the gasworks,
you hit the last and first of London's great upstream
docks, the mile-long twin expanses of the Royals. See
them before they are developed; on a summer's day, they
provide a totally unexpected expanse of deep blue water
rippled by the wind, almost like an inland sea. This is
where London will soon have its fourth airport. Within a
couple of years, short-haul planes will leave there for
Paris and other European cities, all linked by rapid transit
to the City. But so vast are the Royals that it will take
more than an airport to replace the economic activity that
used to go with the port traffic.

To the north of the Royals are some of east London's
neatest housing, the kind that would fetch £70,000 in
Fulham but much less here. Mind you, east London
prices are going up. Young City workers have discovered
artisans' cottages in Stratford and Leytonstone, from
where it is easy to commute west. Estate agents from west
London are now becoming attracted by the east. They are
not, yet, interested in what you can see from the sea-wall
at the Royals. Across the river is a tangle of bushes, trees,
and open land on the southern shore. This is an old
artillery dump which for those fortunate enough to be
allowed in is one of the great nature reserves of London.
Eventually, if all goes according to plan – though plans
are constantly changing – it will be part of Thamesmead,
the GLC-designed new town, scheduled to have a
population of 40,000. Thamesmead is at once depressing
and exhilarating. Depressing, because the first homes
built there are in the tower and deck-access blocks that no
one wants to live in – getting tenants to move there in the
early 1970s, when the development was first opened, was
almost impossible. Depressing, too, for the number of

squalid gypsy sites that you can often see on its edges, a testimony of sorts to the failure of most local authorities to provide decent camping grounds for travellers. Exhilarating because of its site on the river bank – marred only by a sewage works, but you can't have everything – and for the excellent new housing that private developers have constructed, with the GLC's co-operation, in the last few years. If the ownership of Thamesmead after the demise of the Greater London Council can be sorted out – and local political squabbles have not made that easy – it could be a nice place to live. Few would have predicted that five years ago.

From Thamesmead you can see the silver canopies of the Thames flood barrier, and behind it the largely uninteresting terraces of Charlton. But up the hill, to the south, things get very interesting indeed as you hit Blackheath, another of London's genuine villages, and, below it, the incomparable group of seventeenth- and eighteenth-century buildings around the Naval College at Greenwich, with contributions by Inigo Jones, Wren and Vanbrugh. Typically for London, you are now back at the borders of Crescent, indeed hard by some of its most depressing streets. If contrasts are what make a city tick, London has plenty of them.

3
HOME

Mark and Lucy in Balham have one. Nick and Roz in Baron's Court have one. Tony and Julie in Denmark Hill have one; so do John and Lynne, who've got one in Battersea (they used to have one in Queen's Park). The great London institution is the great London house, and the great London house is neither a depressing flat in an East End council estate, nor a grand "white" building in Kensington or Belgravia. It is the late Victorian and Edwardian terrace, and the areas listed above are some of the best places to see this singular London phenomenon.

Of course, there are terraces in other British towns, as in European and American ones, but the huge area covered by London's terraces, and the diversity of the houses within it, is such as to constitute a distinct form of housing. The number of those terraces is to a large extent a function of the remarkable growth in the population of London in the latter half of the nineteenth century. In 1841 "inner London" – the area of the old London county – had a population of about 2m. By 1901 it had over 4.5m (it has never been as high as that since). Greater London in 1841 had about 2.2m people; by 1901, three times as many. The rate of increase between inner and outer areas started to diverge around the 1870s; from then on, the outer ring grew faster than inner London, until Greater London as a whole hit its peak of 8.6m in 1939. There has been a population loss of nearly 2m since then.

The nineteenth-century growth in population was itself the function of London's attraction for those who lived in the surrounding countryside, the rest of the country, and who came from overseas. It was the late nineteenth-century that saw one of the largest waves of immigration; this was the time, for example, that east European Jews moved into the East End. To this "magnet" effect has to be added the impact of the great period of Victorian railway building. The railways both solved and created a housing problem. The one that they created was the dispersal of those who lived in some of London's worst slums – those cleared, for example, for the lines that come into Euston, St Pancras and King's Cross, the three termini within half a mile of each other along the northern boundary of Park and City. The working-class inhabitants of those areas had to go somewhere; all too often, that somewhere was to nearby, already overcrowded slums, which quickly became worse still. (The area abutting onto those three termini is to this day pretty nasty, albeit no more than a short walk from the heart of the West End).

The problem that the railways solved was the housing of those who had either escaped from the slums of inner London, or, more likely, who had been attracted to the capital from outside. From the 1860s to the 1930s, railway companies worked hand in glove with developers. A ready market of commuters helped the profits of the railway company and a ready market of house-buyers or renters swelled those of the land developers. In the twentieth century, this mutual backscratching led to the relatively spacious developments in Metroland, or, perhaps the most famous result of the developer/railway partnership of all, in Golders Green. In the nineteenth century it led to the London terrace.

Many of those terraces were built to designs from the great "style-books"; as the books had a variety of different designs, the terraces themselves avoided a stifling appearance of "sameness". The street where I live in west London, for example, has four distinct styles of terraced houses within 300 yards, each built at roughly five-year intervals between 1875 and 1890. To the inbuilt variety that flowed from the style-books, London's builders and, in particular, their stonemasons, added their own idiosyncratic touches. Walk through any part of Brookstown, or Crescent, or Micawber, and you will see houses that, though clearly similar, have little and not-so-little distinguishing features. One will have a bow window; one a square one. One will have cornices on the roof, one will be plain. Some of the best terraces will have carved fruit and flowers adorning the front of each house. Go inside and you will see yet more differences – in the layout of the rooms (some, for example, were built with the two main ground-floor rooms connected by a folding door, others with a dividing wall) or in the mouldings, fireplaces or tilework.

These little touches are just what the gentrifier of Brookstown loves, because they give him or her the opportunity to create their own little dream home; besides, these features give a house a patina of authenticity, and that is a very prized quality in Brookstown. Thus estate agents' blurbs will always say if a house has its original features – its fireplaces, its cornices, its carved angels in the hall. But these features alone would not make the London terraces the great attraction they have become. What gives them added bite is the feeling of both spaciousness and adaptability that those who wrote and worked from the style-books managed to put into their creation.

Why spacious and adaptable? Probably because of a feature of many of London's terraces identified for me by an old woman who once read my coffee-grains in Istanbul. "You", she said, "live in a house that has two stories at the front and three at the back". And indeed I do. Those three stories – the "back addition" in building jargon – are what give the London terrace its peculiar flavour. It means that the house is full of half-landings; you walk up a short flight of stairs to one or two rooms, turn through 180 degrees and go up another flight, and so on to a room or two at the top of the house, once designed for servants. That both gives the impression that a house is bigger than it really is – a four-bedroom terraced house, for example, might have five or even six "layers" – and means that the enterprising gentrifier can ring the changes over the uses to which he puts each room. Some will have the main sitting-room on the first floor (or third "layer"), some on the ground floor; some will clear out all the rooms on the ground floor of the back addition to make one big kitchen, some will keep a scullery and a smaller workplace, and so on and so on. From the outside, the houses of those friends of mine listed at the beginning of this chapter look almost the same (though not quite, for which thank the stonemasons). Inside, each is completely individual.

This frenetic individualising of the London terrace takes both time and effort. Those walking through London will notice this activity first by the constant presence throughout Brookstown, and many other parts of the city, of the most ubiquitous symbol of the new London – the skip. A skip is an ugly trapezoid box of cast iron, some five feet high and, at its base, about ten feet long, which builders deposit outside a house that is being done up. Into the skip goes all the detritus of the Victorian builder's trade – like old lath-and-plaster – plus such of those additions to the house made by recent working-class residents which the new gentrifiers think detract from its authenticity. So out go the frosted glass doors; out go the polystyrene ceiling tiles; out go the 1950s and 1960s gas fires with imitation logs. In come new doors, rescued from some builders' yard, or bought new, at great expense; in come the old fireplaces; in come the fitted kitchens – authenticity should not be taken too far, especially in the kitchen.

It goes without saying that this activity costs money; lots of it. If there is one thing that those who live outside London cannot understand about those who live in it, it is the price they are prepared to pay for their houses. A terraced house in Brookstown can cost at least four times as much as a similar one in Manchester or Birmingham.

The smart Londoner knows that, but knows also that the London house market gives plenty of scope for making lots of cash – or at least it has done so for most of the last 25 years. London is so huge, that, from the 1960s, when gentrification first became a game anyone could play, different parts of the city have become fashionable at different times. The smart house-buyer bought in Camden Town in the 1960s, sold at a whopping profit at the start of the 1970s, bought a bigger house in Clapham and has just sold that and retired to Downland where he can afford a couple of acres and a pony for the children. Stories of the amount of money that people have made on this merry-go-round are the most boring topic of conversation at a London dinner-table. To get a few out of the way, let us note the people who bought a run-down house in Chiswick for £20,000 in 1977, did it up, and could now sell it for close to £200,000. Or those (not many, but there were some) who bought East End properties a decade ago which they could now sell for a profit, discounted for inflation, of perhaps 500%. It hasn't been plain sailing all the way; the great property boom of 1972 and 1973, when prices doubled in six months, was followed by a nearly as dramatic slump. Prices probably fell, in real terms, throughout the latter half of the 1970s. But they are taking off again now (at a rate of more than 12% a year – much more in the East End). Over 25 years, London's houses have represented one of the most surefire capital-appreciating assets in the whole British economy.

"Yes, but", a querulous logician might say, "I can see that London's house prices have gone up – but why? OK, the stock of housing is relatively stable, and not much new building has happened in the last decade. But the population of London is falling, for God's sake. So simple supply and demand can't explain the price rises".

Simple supply and demand doesn't. To see what does, it is first necessary to remember that those who work in Park and City are the richest Britons of all. They want space – more space than their parents would have thought necessary – and they are prepared to pay for it. What is more, they have to pay for it. The rented housing sector in London, as in Britain as a whole, has been declining since 1914. Its decline was hastened by rent control legislation brought in by Labour governments in the 1960s and 1970s. Seeing their already meagre rates of return squeezed yet further, small and not-so-small landlords simply sold up. If you want a biggish house (say, three bedrooms or more) in London, that you think you'd like to live in for some time, and you've got some disposable cash, you have no alternative – you *have* to buy.

Does that not mean that Londoners are mortgaged up to the hilt? Yes, it does, or at least it does for those who have not been cute enough to play the geographical market described above. But that has acted as less of a drag on the housing market than many would suppose. Getting capital for house purchases in London has been transformed since the early 1970s, when the building societies started to take into account two salaries (if a family had them) when calculating the size of mortgage that people could afford. That meant that young married couples, both, say, with jobs in Park and City, could borrow (for example – precise rules change all the time) one-and-a-half times their joint salaries. That is a lot of potatoes to put into property.

And it gets better. For some of the most perceptive observers of London's terraced houses have noticed that their status as the great British capital asset is now 25 years old. That is significant. It means that today's house buyers have parents who already own houses that have appreciated during the two decades or so they have owned them. So they have yet more cash to lend to their children; or they may have died already, in which case they have left behind a pile of capital unthinkable in the 1950s. One way or another, London is becoming a very capital-rich city indeed. As long as bricks and mortar are

a more favoured investment for the British than stocks
and shares, expect the London house market to keep on
rising.

There is one other reason for the amount of cash that
Londoners are prepared to sink into their terraced houses,
which has nothing to do with money at all. "The
English", says Frances Cairncross, an acute analyst of
housing in Britain, "hate flats". But plenty of them have
no choice. Which leads us to the consideration of another
part of the story of London's homes, one a good deal more
depressing than the hundred-year history of the late
Victorian terrace.

The public housing problem
Virtually every official projection of London's population
since 1945 has been wrong, which makes any guess made
in this book remarkably foolhardy. Still, there is no harm
in having a go. Most present estimates suggest that
London's population will decline only a little from 6.7m
during the next 20 years. But careful work by the GLC
indicates that the number of households in London will
continue to rise. GLC analysts think that the growth of
one-parent families and single-person households means
that the total number of households will grow from its
present level of 2.7m to about 2.8m by the early 1990s. At
first glance, that does not necessarily suggest an
upcoming crisis. London has about 2.7m dwellings now.
A reasonable construction programme, you might think,
would easily be able to mop up the pool of new
households entering the market.

Things are not that simple, for three reasons. First,
London's housing needs more spent on it than that of
most other areas in Britain. More of it is old, more of it
overcrowded. Nearly 19% of London's dwellings were
built before 1890, as compared with only 13% in the rest
of south-east England, and 16% in the rest of England and
Wales. In London, 35% of all dwellings were built after

1945 (though only 11% after 1970). In the rest of the south-east, 67% were built after the war, over 17% since 1970; in England and Wales, 51% of dwellings have been built since 1945, 16% since 1970.

There is no necessary correlation between the age of a dwelling and its state of unfitness. Yet for whatever reason there is no doubt that London's dwellings need a lot of work. In 1981, 5% of Londoners lived more than one to a room, compared with a national average of 3%. In London, 7% of households lacked exclusive use of a bath, or didn't have an indoor lavatory – that applied to only 4% of households nationally. In all, the GLC reckons that in inner London 31% of all dwellings are unsatisfactory (21% of public-sector dwellings and 42% of private-sector ones) while 20% of outer London dwellings are similarly unsatisfactory. Predictably, it is the Crescent boroughs of Hackney, Newham, Tower Hamlets and Lambeth that are worst hit. They head the government's league table of local authorities with housing problems.

The second reason why the apparently simple match of dwellings and households masks a genuine problem is the decline of investment in housing. Housing was a hot political issue in Britain in the 1960s and was addressed, albeit in fairly disastrous ways (of which more later), by the governments of the 1960s and early 1970s. This led some who should have known better to assume that the problem was solved. Thus when the present, Conservative, government took power in 1979, the housing budget was one of the targets for its cost-cutting measures. Most of that budget is spent by local councils (in London, by the borough councils, though the GLC always had a housing role as well) on the authority of central government. And the housing thus built is then rented to households – thus giving the "council housing" of which we spoke in Chapter 1. According to the GLC, investment in new house-building for rent by local authorities in London was under £160m in 1983-84, only 13% (in 1983-84 prices) of what it was in 1975. Translated into new building "starts", that means that in 1975 over 28,000 dwellings (in both the public and private sector) were started, but only 12,600 in 1984. Within that total there has been a slight increase in the amount of private-sector activity, but nothing like enough to have an impact on the total picture. Private-sector house starts, for example, increased from 2,100 in 1975 to 4,100 in 1984; flat starts increased from 3,350 to 3,900 in the same period.

The third reason why you can't match the numbers of households and dwellings and assume that everything is fine is the make-up of those households. London still has the magnet function that it had in the nineteenth-century. Young single people still want to live there, but find that there is a shortage of the kind of dwellings they would like. Similar findings are made by old single people, by those recently arrived from abroad, and by single-parent families – and all these groups are over-represented in London as compared with Britain as a whole. Part of the difficulty comes from the fact that historically, and perhaps for good reasons, public housing authorities have concentrated on housing "traditional" families. But the consequence is that London has a mismatch between the kind of dwellings that exist in the capital and the kind of households there.

Traditionally (by which, in this case, one really means in the nineteenth century) this mismatch was solved by the private rented sector, which provided homes for those who did not fit the priorities of local authorities and who could not afford to buy their own houses. The disastrous decline of the private rented housing sector since 1914 has thus made the problem much worse than it needs to be. Even where private rented housing still exists, the rate of return on capital employed in it is so small that necessary repairs and improvements to homes are often not done. The worst housing conditions in London are now to be found in that sector, with gross overcrowding, evasion of fair-rent and security of tenure laws, and plenty of examples of the practice called "Rachmanism" in the 1960s. Rachman was a particularly unscrupulous landlord who used heavy mobs to force tenants to pay more than they should, at the pain of having their belongings thrown into the street. There are plenty of little Rachmans still around, preying, particularly, on new immigrant communities.

It is little comfort to those who have to live with the difficulties caused by the housing market in London, but they are at least not new. There has hardly been a book written or study made of the city for the last 150 years that has not identified housing as its major social problem. In the mid-nineteenth century, the problem turned on what to do with the overcrowded, noisome and unhealthy slums, portrayed so evocatively in the novels of Dickens, that were to be found all over inner London. As we have already seen, the railways did not help, decanting perhaps 100,000 slum-dwellers into yet more unpleasant neighbouring areas. Into this miasma strode one of London's most interesting social phenomena – and one that is likely to prove as important in the late twentieth century as it was in the late nineteenth – the housing association.

Housing associations were originally charitable bodies whose purpose was to provide housing for the poor. The best known of the nineteenth-century ones was probably the Peabody Trust, which built estates all over the city – good examples can still be seen in Islington and Fulham – and was founded in 1862 by an American philanthropist. Today the most visible association is the Notting Hill Housing Trust. This is not just because of its estates, though there are plenty of those (most of them in the borough of Kensington & Chelsea where some 15% of all dwellings are owned by housing associations), but because of its ubiquitous fund-raising shops throughout west London. Since 1974, a national body, the Housing Corporation, has partially funded the associations, but they raise additional funds themselves and then give

"nomination rights" to their local boroughs – meaning
that they fill a certain proportion of their stock from the
borough's waiting list.

The associations have never had a wholly good press.
In their early days, they were often said to make a much
too rigid distinction between the deserving poor (whom
they wanted) and the undeserving poor (whom they
didn't). It was claimed that they were too expensive for
the really desperate poor; and that they imposed all kinds
of petty rules and restrictions on what their tenants could
do. One at least of the criticisms of them was, and
remains, valid. Their great late-nineteenth-century
estates are pretty forbidding, fortress-like structures,
which seem to warn those unable to get a place within
them to stay well away.

Some criticisms of the associations are still heard
today. Some of London's more radical housing pressure
groups think that they are no better than any other private
landlord, that they do not tolerate the really hard-up
tenant, and that they still nanny people too much. Well, I
may be biased – some of my best friends work for housing
associations – but I think they do a great job, and, more to
the point, a job that London is going to need more of, not
less.

Why place so much faith in the housing associations?
Principally, because they have shown themselves to be
flexible and adaptable. They have provided homes for
some of those groups (like single people) left behind by
other forms of tenure, and they have shown themselves
willing and able to attract private capital to augment their
own resources. None of those achievements has proved
within the easy reach of borough councils.

That does not mean that council housing has no place
in the London of the future. For one thing, the council
housing stock is so extensive that even with right-to-buy
legislation in place there will be many thousands of
households paying rent to local authorities for many
years. In Britain as a whole, about 26% of the housing

stock is in the public sector. In London the figure is higher – 35% – but this masks some remarkable differences between the boroughs. In outer London, the eastern boroughs of Barking & Dagenham and Greenwich have 58% and 51% respectively of their dwellings in the public sector, but the average in outer London is much lower – only 25%. Harrow has only 14%; Redbridge (at the northern edge of New Bow Bells) 15%, while a Waterside borough like Richmond has 17%. Contrast that with the figures in inner London. The lowest proportion of public housing – at 26% – is in Kensington & Chelsea. The boroughs in Crescent have quite extraordinary figures. Islington has 66% of its housing in the public sector, Hackney has 70%. Southwark has 75% (Simon Hughes, the MP for Southwark Bermondsey, on the river, once told me that he reckoned that only 3% of his constituents were home owners), and the borough of Tower Hamlets, immediately to the east of the City, has an almost unbelievable 86% of its dwellings in public ownership.

This vast municipal estate sprang from two sources. The first was high altruism; the second low politics. The altruism started when Victorian and Edwardian social reformers realised that neither private housebuilding nor the charitable trusts could mop up all those displaced from inner-London slums. So the London County Council (LCC), created in 1889, built homes for the needy, starting with three hostels, for men only, built between 1893 and 1906. Acts of Parliament (of which the first was the Housing of the Working Classes Act in 1890) then progressively gave more home-building powers to the County Council and the old borough councils. The LCC dwarfed the boroughs. By 1938 it had built nearly 87,000 dwellings, creating, while doing so, some new towns from almost virgin land. Becontree, in New Bow Bells, had 26,000 homes and a population that rapidly grew to 120,000. About 60% of pre-war LCC housing was in blocks of flats, of which plenty are still visible throughout

Crescent. Most of them are four or five storeys high, with a distinctive mock English-rustic look. Their external appearance, at least, has worn tolerably well — much better, at any rate, that what followed.

For the post-war years brought new problems. The slum clearance programme was made more difficult by bomb damage. Over 10% of the LCC's dwellings had been destroyed or rendered totally uninhabitable by enemy action. Virgin land was now unobtainable, so new housing had to be built on the sites of old. In one of the oldest of all London cliches, but true for all that, what the bombers had started, government planners completed. Great swathes of the East End were demolished and new housing constructed. But all too often these buildings were slim tower blocks ("point" blocks, in the trade) or not quite so tall "slab" blocks built with grandiose streets in the sky – "deck-access", as it is known. The new blocks were ushered in with a fanfare. The Roehampton Vale estate was based on designs inspired by Le Corbusier, and to be fair, looks tolerable 30 years after it was completed. But when the official history of the LCC said in 1965 that "families enjoyed living up high" and that the towers "added architectural interest to London's skyline" it told a good deal less than the truth. The reality was that penny-pinching and misguided central government subsidies encouraged high blocks, as did a remarkable professional orthodoxy shared by the architects at the LCC and the Ministry of Housing. Later came industrial, "system" building techniques that neither architects nor builders understood, and the result was London's awful post-war estates. As usual, the Crescent came out worst. Hackney has 82 blocks over ten storeys tall, Southwark 81, and Newham 67. Newham has the most famous of all. One morning in 1968, a gas cooker caused an explosion in a Newham system-built tower block called Ronan Point. It collapsed at a corner like a pack of cards, and the true scale of the public housing monster became apparent.

The creation of that monster was both sad and

unnecessary. Many of the small houses in the East End and elsewhere demolished in the 1950s and later could have been saved and rehabilitated, as boroughs like Camden have shown. And that is what most inhabitants wanted. Households have been forced out of their houses and into flats; communities have been split up. Of all the sad statistics in London, none is so mournful as that, in 1976, 66% of those living on GLC estates (mainly old LCC ones) did not know a single neighbour.

It is unfair, and naive, to blame misplaced altruism for the whole of this catastrophe. Grafted on top of unattainable dreams were all too real political calculations. Both the size and the location of the largest, worst maintained, inner-city estates are a function of politics. These estates have always been a source of captive votes for the Labour Party. The boroughs of Tower Hamlets, Islington, Southwark and Hackney between them had, in 1985, only 11 Conservative councillors out of a total of more than 150. There has thus been little effective pressure since the 1950s from Labour politicians to move some of the population of those estates out into the much less densely populated outer boroughs. In this the Conservative-controlled outer boroughs have been happy to connive. They have been able to preserve their largely uncrowded neighbourhoods (housing density in the most crowded outer borough – Brent – is less than that in Newham, the least crowded inner borough). So the inner-city estates and those who live in them stay put.

The real tragedy of this is that most new jobs in London, as we shall see in Chapter 6, are in its outer areas. Public housing in the inner city acts as a trap to those who live there. There is no point in saying that those who live in those estates should exercise their rights under right-to-buy laws and purchase their homes. It is not uncommon, in these inner-city estates, to find that over 50% of the population depends entirely on state support for its income. Even if inhabitants could afford to buy their flats, they could not afford to refurbish them so that they were saleable. Even if they had the necessary money, who would buy an oasis-like flat in an estate which was almost utterly desolate?

Not all is grim. Take, as an example, Broadwater Farm in Tottenham, now perhaps the most notorious of all London's modern estates. This was the scene of the pitched battle between the police and mainly black youngsters in October, 1985, during which Constable Keith Blakelock was killed. The Farm has 1,100 dwellings, in both tower and deck-access blocks, which were first occupied in the early 1970s. It has one common feature of the worst designed estates – the curious assumption that nobody ever wants to live or walk on the ground floor. The Farm is built wholly on stilts; everything under them is a wasteland, and this ground floor area is linked to the first storey by narrow staircases with sharp bends, round each of which a determined mugger can lurk unseen. The shops on the estate are wholly inadequate to the needs of its population, and were so long before the riot gutted the only, small, supermarket. More than half the Farm is black and perhaps 40% of its young people are unemployed. Well over half the households on the estate depend on state benefits for their income. The Farm has four entrances from neighbouring terraced streets; no through traffic goes through it and access to the pleasant park that lies behind it is not easy. It is a world of its own.

And a pretty awful one, it might seem. Yet there is a remarkable community spirit on the Farm. At public meetings after the riot, some local politicians argued that its problems could only be solved by demolition. This brought howls of protest from many of those who lived there, white as well as black. An outstanding black woman, Mrs Dolly Kiffin, started a Youth Association some years ago which provides meals for the elderly, and which now runs some co-operative shops – a hairdresser and a launderette are already in place (they were untouched in the riot) and others are planned. The local borough, Haringey, which is a favourite whipping-boy for Britain's right-wing press, has taken its responsibilities on the estate very seriously indeed. All management matters are now handled by a local office there; tenants do not need to trek to the civic centre in Wood Green High Street, a mile away, to sort out repairs, lettings or rent problems. The caretakers of the estate cleared it of broken glass and rubbish within 24 hours of the fighting; the neighbourhood office worked day and night to get everything back to normal. As a matter of course, all racist graffiti is removed from walls within a day of its appearance. Central government has helped. The Farm is one of the areas covered by the Department of the Environment's priority estates project and this provides consultancy advice for its problems; some civil servants are convinced that the Farm is one of their real success stories.

I find Broadwater Farm one of the most uplifting places in London. It is evidence of what local people can do when they are encouraged to think that they can solve a problem for themselves; and it is evidence, especially, that good housing management, with services decentralised to estates, can turn a "sink" estate into one that people have affection for. Ideally, it would be possible to go further, by handing some estates over to companies owned by their tenants, though attempts to do this outside London have not so far met with much success. Another approach might be to set up housing trusts with mixed private and public-sector funding. This is the course that has been chosen at Thamesmead, London's very own new town, on land south of the river and east of Greenwich. Like Broadwater Farm, its first dwellings were occupied in the early 1970s; these too in tower and deck-access blocks. They were, predictably, hard to let and fell into decay. The GLC, which owned the estate, then invited private builders in; they have now laid out some really delightful streets, all with easy access to water. Now that the GLC has gone, the trust will try to manage the estate (there is still plenty of land for building) until it turns into a town-within-a-town of 40,000 people. Like Broadwater Farm, it is a heartening example of what good management and a lack of political dogma (it was, after all, the Labour-controlled GLC that most encouraged private developers at Thamesmead) can achieve.

It is only realistic to add some caveats to this more optimistic picture of the possibilities for council housing. Some boroughs have been less assiduous than Haringey in trying to improve the management of their estates. Some – Southwark is an example – have allowed rent arrears to accumulate to such levels that the financial solvency of the borough is threatened. Others, one may surmise, are just not able to cope with the scale of the problems that face them. Tower Hamlets, one of the poorest boroughs, had about 20,000 dwellings in its charge until 1986, and found managing them difficult enough. On the abolition of the GLC, it was then handed another 30,000 properties within its boundaries – many of them some of the oldest public housing blocks in London, built by the LCC and managed on its demise by the GLC. How Tower Hamlets will cope with this enormous housing stock is a prospect that its tenants must view with alarm. The amount of capital spending needed by some boroughs is huge, and the funds that they have been allocated by the government pitifully small. Gentrification through right-to-buy laws, which would be the best way of pulling some estates up, is an awfully long way in the future; virtually no tower or deck-access inner-city flats have been sold to their tenants, and even a decade of enlightened management will not change that picture. Some estates will almost certainly have to come down – indeed, Hackney council has started demolishing some of its worst modern estates in the last year. This is never a wholly satisfactory solution, for it nips in the bud any community spirit that might be developing, and merely shifts the problem elsewhere – shades of

nineteenth-century slum clearance – yet in a few
locations it will be the only possible outcome.

Nice places
The worst public housing estates represent what is bad
about London's housing, and its terraces what is most
interesting. Yet millions of Londoners, of course, live in
neither. For some, indeed, Frances Cairncross's adage
does not hold good. London has plenty of people who do
not mind living in flats at all. Some of its most wealthy
inhabitants are keener on flats than houses; a town flat
can act as an easy-to-manage *pied-à-terre* during the
working week, with its occupants speeding out along the
M4 each Friday to their homes in the country.

Thus although London has, by American standards,
few high-cost high-rise blocks, it does have some. There
are some good examples, for instance, on the ridge
between Archway and Crouch End, at the southern edge
of the Northern Heights, which have splendid views over
the City. (In time, there will almost certainly be more
buildings of this type along the river; until quite recently,
getting a river view from your home was far from easy.)
But the best known examples of this type of dwelling are
the three towers of the Barbican Centre, at the northern
boundary of the City. This site was devastated during the
Second World War and later compulsorily purchased by
the City Corporation, an ancient (and some would say
anachronistic) local government unit that runs the
financial square mile. The 400-foot high tower blocks
were built in the 1960s and, though there have always
been attempts to woo those with low or moderate
incomes into the development, its typical owner remains
the city banker or accountant, or the politician – people,
in any case, who either do not like staying in London over
the weekend or who have no need to.

The Barbican has never been over-popular either with
residents or with other Londoners. At first, the towers

seemed like three dragon's teeth on the skyline. This
aspect of the development's image has been saved by the
number of high-rises that have invaded the City in the last
15 years. Where once the Barbican towers stood alone,
they now form one part of a cluster of skyscrapers that can
look quite appealing from afar. But the flats there are
quite small and cramped, and not cheap. Moreover, at
least until the Barbican arts centre was opened in 1982,
the whole area felt horribly artificial and lifeless. It still
has no real sense of community; no higgledy-piggledy
shops and pubs of the kind that give many of London's
neighbourhoods their lifeblood. City chaps, evidently,
don't worry about that.

Much more attractive than the Barbican are the groups
of late Victorian and Edwardian "mansion flats" seen in
Kensington, Earls Court, elsewhere in inner west
London, and, possibly best of all, along the length of
Prince of Wales Drive, to the south of Battersea Park. Like
the terraces, these are often testaments to the stonema-
son's art. Splendid brickwork, the exuberant use of
terracotta and plaster, and more chimneys than seem
possible combine to create a red and cream mosaic, like a
slab of meat seen through a kaleidoscope. I love these
buildings; at their best, they remind me of the solid
tenements of Glasgow and Edinburgh. They are tough, yet
they have something that more modern blocks of flats
seem frightened of – a sheer delight in decoration for its
own sake. They were once almost all rented from private
landlords, which made them appealing to a transient
population – my mother-in-law knows her way round
South Kensington by the mansion blocks her family lived
in (and were bombed out of) during the 1930s and 1940s.
They are now increasingly in owner occupation. Unlike
the terraced houses, however, owners of mansion flats
usually only have leaseholds, not freeholds, so if you
don't care about leaving something to your children you
can pick up a relative bargain (building society willing,
which it may not be), so long as you are prepared to buy

the fag-end 20 or 30 years of a lease.

A mixed population lives in these mansion blocks; prosperous Kensingtonians, yuppies, old people, students, Commonwealth visitors (it was in mansion flats that Aussies settled during the 1960s in Earl's Court, when the area became known as Kangaroo Valley). They are built to a spaciousness that seems almost foreign now; I remember coming close to buying a flat in a block off the Gloucester Road, the living room of which was 40 feet long if it was an inch. Lousy for central-heating bills, worse if you have to club together with everyone else to fix the roof for the first time in 80 years, but these buildings add a solidity to the appearance of London's streets which is never overwhelming or uninteresting.

Some of the "red" mansion blocks have communal gardens and this is a feature, too, of the no less interesting white houses in Notting Hill and Holland Park. These are enormous, but unlike their close relatives in Belgravia, where old money has hung on grimly, many of them are now in multi-ownership (though not left-wing politician Tony Benn's stylish house in Campden Hill Square). This is a fascinating part of London. Despite the fact that the streets leading north up the hill from Holland Park are wider than London's norm, individual gardens were often not provided with the houses. Instead, a patch of land was reserved at the back for all those who abutted on it. Thus are created some of London's most lovely private worlds, ideal for summer parties and barbecues. As late as the 1930s there were some developments built in this way: there is a very odd example of a communal garden behind a triangle of toytown houses in Barton Road, by Barons Court tube station.

For the Englishman's dream of the really spacious garden you usually have to look further out of the centre, though there are exceptions. Houses in St John's Wood, north of Regent's Park, fetch £500,000 and upwards, partly because they have gardens, partly because the proximity of an American school (and the Ambassador's residence) seems to have made it a favourite location for visitors from the United States. Inner suburbs like Ealing have their small, suburban gardens; for the really grand gesture, try The Bishop's Avenue (and never miss out the definite article) which leads from the top of Hampstead Heath to Finchley. This is the closest London gets to a millionaire's row; its houses are massive, and so are their gardens. But ostentation can have its price; there have been some nasty break-ins and murders on the Avenue. (Less objectionable, perhaps, was the huge New Year's party thrown by some anarchists in an empty Avenue house in 1985). By the time you reach Downland and the Northern Heights, gardens may well have given way to paddocks or an acre or two of land. It is space, I suppose, that the English seek when they escape from the city, and the space available in some of London's suburbs (at prices which those who have made a killing inside town can easily afford) is abundant.

And then there are the oddities; the artists' studios, the converted churches and schools. And the houseboats. Most Londoners are only just getting used to the idea that their city is criss-crossed with Victorian waterways, but a few have known it for years. Consider Little Venice where, within a stone's throw of the Westway elevated motorway, and under the noses of a group of tower blocks, Paddington Basin provides the home for a collection of boats. Richard Branson, whizzkid of the Virgin Group, used to live on one, and still uses it as his office. There is another collection at Chelsea Wharf, beneath the council estate at World's End. You have to really love your boat to live there; there's one of London's busiest roads to one side of you and a view, over mud, of a flour mill to the other – I can think of better places. In Covent Garden, meanwhile, there has been a small amount of loft development, though nothing on the scale seen by New Yorkers in recent years. Neal's Yard, a delightful corner with the best wholefood shop in town, an organic bakery and a dairy, and (a bit whimsical, this) an alternative chemist, or apothecary, is the place to see what Covent Garden might have looked like if rents hadn't made it prohibitive for all but commercial uses.

Much more use has been made of old commercial and industrial buildings in dockland. Wapping High Street, to take one example, is lined with fantastic Victorian warehouses. Just five years ago, most of them were boarded up – the only activity around seemed to be discount wine stores. Now the builders are in; the light and airy floors are being turned into flats at prices that mock the incomes of those who have to live in Tower Hamlets council estates just behind the High Street – £300,000 and upwards is not uncommon. South of the river, a consortium is doing up one of the biggest of all warehouses, Butler's Wharf, just east of Tower Bridge. Elsewhere in dockland there is other new housing being built, most of it close to the water.

I suppose all this will work. Some of the people involved in putting up houses in dockland – like Sir Terence Conran, of the Habitat/Mothercare group, who is backing the Butler's Wharf scheme – have a good track record of identifying the tastes of the upwardly mobile. For that matter, David Owen, leader of the Social Democrats, the political party that the upwardly mobile support, has had a house in Limehouse since he was a struggling junior doctor. So why my doubts? I suppose because, although I'm sure that the East End will be the economic success story of the twenty-first century, I think it will be a long time before the fractured community there can provide the shops, pubs and general goodwill that people need to put down roots in a place. Those are things that came naturally in much of Brookstown or Micawber. And, secondly, because one is almost bound to feel uneasy about the clear evidence of such wealth in what is still, mainly, a very poor area. This may be just shortsighted and inconsistent. After all, the gentrification which I maintain is one of the hopes for the worst council estates is already going on in the East End, courtesy, very largely, of warehouse renovation. Certainly for many, the homes being built in dockland are the most exciting housing development for years. For me, I am happy to come home to the quiet, quirky order of a Brookstown terrace.

4
MOVING

I work in the heart of the West End, almost equidistant from Hyde Park Corner, Piccadilly Circus, Trafalgar Square and the Palace of Westminster. A hundred yards from my office runs Piccadilly, one of London's great arterial roads since the early seventeenth century. It is now a one-way street, west to east. I often have to leave the office for the east, and though I am more than happy to take a tube if I can, there are some journeys where surface transport is more convenient or agreeable. You would imagine, then, that I take a bus or a taxi along Piccadilly to some of these eastwards destinations.

I don't, at least hardly ever. One reason is personal preference: weather permitting, I bicycle or walk round central London. But even if I didn't do that, I would still be hard-pressed to use the internal combustion engine along Piccadilly. If I did so between, say, nine o'clock in the morning and six o'clock at night, much of my journey would be spent in a traffic jam. This jam can stretch from Knightsbridge, a mile west of my office, to the far end of Shaftesbury Avenue, a mile east of it. It is one of the best known, and least loved, of all London's bottlenecks, but it is in no sense unique.

Misery
Complaining about traffic is a major pastime in cities all over the world – in Lagos and Mexico City no less than in Paris or New York. In London, it rivals housing as the last refuge of those dinner-parties where nobody knows what to say to their neighbour. And for longer than anyone can remember the city's roads have been a nightmare.

63

Then-and-now photograph books invariably include a late nineteenth-century picture of the Strand, or Oxford Street, or Trafalgar Square, as clogged by horsedrawn traffic then as they are now by cars, buses and lorries. And there are those who would say that things have not, in truth, got much worse in 100 years. Exhaust fumes may be smelly, but any cyclist in London will tell you that even the limited numbers of horses on today's streets produce enough dung to stink to high heaven on a summer's day. A century ago, the smell must have been unbearable.

For most Londoners, comparisons with the distant past are not the point. Traffic congestion, they are convinced, has become worse in the last two decades. The figures confirm this conventional wisdom – traffic levels in London as a whole increased by 15% in the ten years to 1984, though rather more in outer London than in the inner city.

No prizes for guessing why this should be. Private car-ownership tripled in London between 1953 and 1970, and has increased steadily since then; there are now over 2.2m cars in London. In 1981, 68% of households in outer London owned cars; in 1962 only 44%. The same pattern can be seen in inner London; between those dates, car ownership increased from 28% to 44%. But there is something fishy about these figures. In this period the population of London fell, and lots of jobs were lost to the rest of south-east England. These factors have combined to dampen the growth of "classic" commuting. Thus inner Londoners' car journeys declined over the 20 years from 2.17m to 1.13m a day; outer Londoners used the car to get to work less too; their journeys declined from 3.15m to 2.61m.

So why the increased congestion? For three reasons. First, non-work journeys in a car have increased in line with new leisure opportunities and the affluence to enjoy them. In 20 years, these journeys have gone up 19% for inner Londoners, and by 95% – to a total of 4.7m journeys per weekday – for outer Londoners. Second, though the number of journeys to work by car has decreased, their average length has increased. Each car, if you like, is clogging up the roads for longer than it did 25 years ago. Thus the total mileage of journeys to work by car has increased by 28% since 1962, to about 11m miles annually. Third, consider lorry traffic. Though the number of lorries registered in London has increased only marginally in 25 years, the number of heavy lorries – which are what people notice – has doubled. And to lorries should be added the extraordinary growth of private coaches since deregulation of long-distance bus routes in the early 1980s. In some parts of central London, most notably around the Victoria coach terminus, buses now constitute a major traffic problem.

It would be grossly unfair on all those who live in outer London to pretend that the traffic problems of inner London are the only ones worthy of note. It is fairer to say that inner London's congestion needs taking seriously by outer Londoners, because in a critical sense it is the cause of their problem too. To understand that link, it is necessary to go back to the Romans. They were the people who determined that London's road system would be essentially radial in nature. This scheme of things was untouched for 2,000 years – the Great North Road, the Bath Road, the Oxford Road, the Portsmouth Road, and others less important, ran from London's centre like the spokes of a wheel. Once London and the south-east became the motor force of the British economy, this radial pattern began to cause difficulties. Not only was traffic attracted into the centre of town through the outer and inner suburbs, but journeys from one part of the south-east to another all too often involved trekking through London on the way. Until five years ago, it was murder to get from Portsmouth to Ipswich without going through London, or from the north to the Channel without doing the same. Thus once car traffic started to build up in the twentieth century, and especially after

1945, the old high streets of London became jammed; and jammed many of them still are.

Relief
Problem: jammed high streets; solution: by-passes to them. Objection: by-passes through crowded city neighbourhoods (not green fields: many of these problems were not identified until after 1945) mean knocking houses down. So which comes first, homes or roads?

In one manifestation or another, that question has dominated London's politics for 20 years. One of the reasons that the GLC was created in 1963 was to build the new roads that both politicians and civil servants thought essential. The jurisdiction of the old LCC had been limited to Park and City, Crescent and Brookstown. The GLC took in much more; it was thought that only a strategic authority with some powers over suburb as well as city could provide the head-banging needed to build the new roads. Both the Labour and Conservative parties subscribed to this view (though they disagreed over much else to do with the GLC). By the mid-1960s, both were committed to a major road-building plan which was incorporated in the Greater London Development Plan in 1969, by which time the Tories controlled County Hall.

The plan called for three concentric urban motorways, with connecting roads between them. These would have cost (in 1971) between £1,500m and £2,000m. Beyond the city limits was to be an outer orbital motorway. Of all the schemes, the one that caused most fury was the "motorway box", or Ringway 1 – the innermost road. This was designed to run from the end of Westway, north of the city centre to Hackney, where it would join an eastern cross to a new river-crossing. The plan then envisaged a new motorway along the line of the present South Circular Road, running westwards to Battersea. It was the western end of the box that gave so much trouble. From Battersea, a western cross was to run northwards through heavily populated districts (and quite prosperous ones, too) like Chelsea and Earl's Court, until it connected with the Westway at Shepherd's Bush.

Grown men in the Department of Transport turn white to this day when you mention the words "western cross" to them. For what nobody had anticipated happened. From being a moribund lot committed to the belief that socialism could be achieved through public works, the London Labour Party in the late 1960s started to go through the metamorphosis that in 1981 would put Ken Livingstone into power. Influenced partly by the 1960s environmental movement, and largely by political opportunism, the party decided to put homes before roads and forged an alliance with the many community groups who thought that the Ringways were a nonsense – well, worse than that, they thought the Ringways would destroy their homes and neighbourhoods, and in many cases they were right. Labour swept to power in the 1973 GLC elections, and dumped the Ringways. This placed the Tories nicely in the horns of a dilemma. They were hardly going to win County Hall back on the slogan "roads before homes". So during the mid-1970s, the Conservatives edged little by little away from the road-building programme. The Labour Party never shifted; under Livingstone, its policy was clear. In 1984, its proposed modifications to the development plan spelt out Labour's position: "The road-building option unfairly benefits certain groups to the clear disadvantage of others. Private cars are only available to limited sections of our society. Communities have been blighted for many years by the safeguarding of routes for new roads. Quite apart from unacceptably disruptive environmental effects, major road-building is unrealistic in financial terms. The GLC firmly rejects this option." But the GLC was too late. Appalled by the inability to get the roads that they were convinced were necessary, national government civil servants and politicians had long since started plotting the abolition of the GLC itself.

This doleful tale needs something of a gloss. Some roads were indeed built. In east London the environmentalists were less strong, the land was less expensive, and the benefits of new roads for the regeneration of dockland more clearly understood. So, though most people outside east London have not yet realised it, the eastern cross is almost complete. A road is now being built from Redbridge to Barking. This will provide dual-carriageway access from the eastern edge of dockland to the M25, and thence northwards to the expanded airport at Stansted. If the Department of Transport gets its way (the GLC, now out of the picture, did its best to see that it wouldn't) this will be extended southwards across the river by means of a new east London river crossing (Elric) to Falconbridge. The dual-carriageway will then connect with the A20 and A2, both of which are being upgraded; the new A20 will create a much needed by-pass for Sidcup. These roads will provide a link from east London to the channel ports. In addition, a firm line has now been fixed for a road that will link the M11, at the north-east of London, to the Blackwall Tunnel, at the western edge of dockland. Both ends of dockland will thus be tethered to the national motorway network. Moreover, the transport department has been quietly upgrading both the North Circular Road and the western approach to it from Oxford. By the early 1990s, it will be possible to travel on "grade separated" roads (which means that you won't have to bother with traffic lights) from Oxford, onto the A40, round the huge roundabout at Hanger Lane, onto the North Circular, and right round the top of London to the Redbridge-to-Barking road; then (Elric permitting) to the Channel. There will, finally, be one route that takes traffic through London without polluting neighbourhood streets.

All this has been going on with little public attention. What has been noticed is the M25; the "outer orbital" motorway of the development plan. By the time it is finished in the summer of 1986, its 121 miles will constitute the longest orbital motorway in the world. It is already having a profound effect on movement around London, and on the location of economic activity in the city.

Some of these effects are more welcome than others. Consider the good ones first. Early estimates that the M25 would bring immediate overall traffic relief to London of 3.5% over 24 hours now look slightly pessimistic. At the peak morning rush hour, the improvement is more likely to be of the order of 5%, though outer London will naturally benefit more than the inner city. Lorry traffic will decline more than cars; by some 9% during the morning peak, and perhaps by nearly 30% at night. It is now possible to travel from one part of the south-east to another without going through London, and there is an easy road link between the three airports; Heathrow at the west, Gatwick at the south, and Stansted in Essex, north-east of London.

The success of the M25 has brought problems, too. Some of its sections are already overloaded; like all British motorways, most of it is only three lanes wide in each direction. The quadrant between Heathrow and the junction with the M23, north of Gatwick, has already seen major tailbacks; on the southern section, fog has turned these into horrible accidents. Some of the junctions between feeder roads and the motorway get clogged. The difficulty is not as serious as on Paris's *périphérique,* which is much closer to the city centre, and has its feeder roads much closer together, but it is bad enough. Some motorists and their spokesmen have already asked for the M25 to be improved: a bad pinchpoint has developed to the east. The M25 crosses the Thames by means of a tunnel at Dartmouth, constructed not by the Department of Transport but by Kent and Essex county councils. To recoup their investment, they made the tunnel toll-paying. This means that at times of high density, tailbacks form at the toll-booths. The problem will only be solved if central government writes off the counties' debt, thus making the tunnel toll-free, or alternatively gives the go-ahead to a proposed privately financed second tunnel.

The M25 is not the source only of traffic management problems. Its real impact is on the location of industry and commerce. This was an aspect of its construction which few had thought through before the first sod was cut. We have already seen that the M25 places the concept of a "green belt" round London under great pressure. Modern factories and warehouses tend to be low-rise; they need space for fork-lift trucks to whizz round inside their walls, and heavy lorries to draw up outside them. Dockland apart, the obvious place for developments like those close to the national motorway network is along the M25. Hypermarkets and retail malls would like to follow; so would leisure activities and housing. This is leading to much hand-wringing among the county councils through whose leafy acres the M25 runs. Their job of striking a balance between the developers and their inhabitants is difficult enough; but London's politicians face difficult times too, as the GLC noted in 1982. Changes following the completion of the motorway, it said, would "be consistent with the broad trends of recent decades, favouring outer London rather than inner London, and west London rather than east London. In inner London the forces causing long-term decline of industry will be strengthened by the M25". In Chapters 5 and 6 we look at this issue in more detail. For the moment, note merely that to change the way that people move around London is to change the kind of city it will be, and the kind of things that go on within its limits.

There may be other new roads in addition to the M25. Now the GLC has gone, the Department of Transport has taken responsibility for the 65 miles of strategic roads within London that Ken Livingstone and his predecessors looked after. It has thus become possible to build those parts of the Ringway scheme that are still thought to be needed. Is that what is going to happen? Not according to the Department. In May 1985, Lynda Chalker, then the

Transport minister, said that she had no grandiose road plans, and did not propose any revival of the motorway box or ringways. Any solutions to London's problems, she said, "must mean paying careful attention to historical and environmental considerations". Churlishly, the GLC didn't believe a word. For in November 1984, Mrs Chalker had asked consultants to prepare "assessment studies" on four corridors through London which were among the most congested routes in the city. The results of these studies are expected in late 1986. The GLC said they would mean new grade-separated roads; the Department said they were all about transport management – easier traffic flows, better traffic lights, some changes at junctions and the like.

The first of the corridors is, unsurprisingly, the South Circular Road, from Woolwich to Wandsworth. The South Circular is not really a road at all; it is a collection of inner-suburban high streets dignified with a grand title. At present, local traffic along it cannot be separated from through traffic. It is hated both by those who live near it and by those who have to drive along it for any length. The Department of Transport assures anyone who cares to ask that there is no possibility of building a grade-separated road there, as is being done on the line of the North Circular. It would be much too costly – perhaps more than £10m a mile – mainly because of the number of houses that would have to be demolished, with compensation for their owners. Cost aside, no road could be built unless the environmentalists and neighbourhood groups sat idly by and watched the diggers. No chance. There would be court cases, long public inquiries, direct action, and much else. A dual-carriageway along the South Circular is not politically possible, and the sooner everybody realises that, the sooner they may come to accept the changes – like a few flyovers and tunnels at key junctions – that would relieve a lot of the pressure.

The second corridor is no easier. This stretches from Wandsworth along the South Circular through Putney and Sheen, around Chalker's Corner (not named after the erstwhile minister) across Kew Bridge and up to the worst part of the North Circular, which runs through Ealing to the junction with the Oxford motorway at Hanger Lane. This has some scope for road widening and for flyovers (but only at the cost, for example, of spoiling Ealing Common) but the same problems with local environmentalists as the first corridor, should anything bigger be attempted. This west London study also includes "an exploration in detail of the possibility of constructing a relief road for the Earl's Court one-way system by dual use of the existing railway corridor". Very sensible, you say. There is indeed a railway corridor that runs from Shepherd's Bush, at the end of the Westway, through Earl's Court towards the river. What could be simpler than to put a road along it as well?

But the careful reader will have noted that this is a sensitive area. "Oh", I once said to civil servants at the Department of Transport, "You're finally going to build the western cross". "No, no, no", they shrieked. But if not that, what are they going to do? It's all very well using the railway corridor, but that only goes as far as the river. Thus traffic coming down it from the Westway will either pile off the new road at Cheyne Walk in Chelsea, and go along the Embankment, which is already chock-a-block, and peopled by those who don't take kindly to juggernauts outside their front doors, or a new high-level bridge will have to be built to Battersea and thus link with the South Circular. But Battersea has high-density housing, much of it newly gentrified. My guess is that the environmentalists will kybosh this one too.

They may have less success in Corridor Three, because it goes through an area where they have been less strong. This is the district to the north-east of the City, from Islington through Hackney. The problem here is that traffic coming along the Marylebone Road from the west and heading north or east now has to go into the heart of the City before it can get out again. A road that linked dockland to the Great North and Cambridge roads is thus thought to be important. I wonder. The road schemes already under way in dockland link it to the M25, from which access to the north of England is easy. And traffic from the west to the east is, presumably, intended to use the North Circular. So why, apart from the fact that it was on the Ringway plan, attempt to provide an extra link? Still, property prices here are lower (as long as the City does not spread its high rents northwards) and the inhabitants are still mainly working-class and have not yet been environmentalised to the same extent as elsewhere. The prospects for new roads look quite good.

Better, at least, than they do in Corridor Four, which goes along the Brighton road from the end of the M23, north of Gatwick airport, past Croydon to the heart of Micawber. A few years ago, the Department of Transport bought pockets of land along this corridor, expecting to extend the M23 to Tooting Common. But public expenditure cuts stopped the plan; most of that land has been sold. House prices have risen and to get the land back would cost the earth. Even civil servants accept that there is no chance of the motorway now. They are looking for the same kind of traffic management schemes as on the South Circular. Purley Way, around Croydon, for example, needs some environmentally benign upgrading.

On balance, I think the GLC was unkind to Mrs Chalker. The political realities make major road-building in much of inner London impossible without oodles of money. The time horizon for most projects makes them no more than a gleam in a traffic engineer's eye. At the same time, the Department has changed its view of what is both possible and desirable. London's traffic will never be light. But nor, I think, will the city be blighted by the thought or prospect that just round the corner are six-lane motorways. The tension between environmentalists and traffic planners will always be uneasy; but the stand-off they have now reached, to which the key is an acceptance of substantial traffic management schemes, is one that in the long run might suit both sides well.

Hot air

Though not part of Mrs Chalker's studies, a fifth corridor
is also being looked at. This is the road link from
Heathrow airport to central London. By the standards of
most gateways to London, the roads from the west should
be a paradise. The M4 and M40 take traffic as far as
Chiswick and Ealing respectively. From there, few traffic
lights slow up the trip to the centre of town. Yet both
arteries are a misery. The M4 and its continuation into the
Great West and Cromwell Roads is particularly bad. At
times, traffic can move at no more than a crawl from
Chiswick to Piccadilly.

One reason for the tailbacks is the remarkable growth of
Heathrow airport. In 1950 all UK airports handled only
2m passengers. In 1985 Heathrow alone handled 30m.
Terminal Four, opened in 1986, will push the capacity up
to 38m, and there may be more on the way. The
government's White Paper on airport policy in 1985 said
that the removal of the sludge works to the west of the
airport was highly desirable. This would clear the way for
Terminal Five (to which the government is not
committed, but which British Airways desperately
wants) thus pushing the capacity up to around 50m
passengers a year. That is more than any airport in the
world has now.

These figures, and the environmental difficulties that
they inevitably bring, have made a 30-year nightmare out
of the search for a consensus on a policy for London's
airports. The 1985 White Paper, and the report of an
inquiry by Mr Reginald Eyre on which it was based, are
widely thought to have come closer to getting things right
than any other attempt. In a sense, the dilemma is a nice
one. Aeroplanes are the one form of transport in which
the fact that Britain is an island is not a disadvantage.
Speaking English positively helps in this most interna-

tional of all industries. And in recent years, the passion of the British for foreign holidays has boosted demand for seats on planes; the growth of demand for air traffic in the south-east was inevitable.

The south-east, in this context, has traditionally meant Heathrow or Gatwick. Gatwick is some 15 miles south of Croydon, and was opened in 1958 to relieve pressure on Heathrow. If any airport can be called lovely, Gatwick is. A fast railway links it with Victoria, and from Gatwick's own train station it is only a short walk to the booking-halls. Heathrow, by contrast, requires either a slow journey by tube or an even slower one by bus; or an absurdly expensive, and just as slow, taxi. Though often thought to be mainly a charter airport, Gatwick now mainly services scheduled flights, partly because the British Airports Authority has been sending foreign carriers to Gatwick from overcrowded Heathrow. Its capacity is at present about 14m passengers a year. A new terminal now under construction will boost the figure to about 25m. That will be the lot. The government has accepted that environmental considerations rule out a second runway on the site.

The dilemma now begins to take shape. Say there is no fifth terminal at Heathrow. Then capacity at the two main airports will be something in the order of 61m passengers a year – the figure that Mr Eyre concluded was the likely demand for flights in 1990. By 1995 he thought there would need to be capacity for 75m passengers, and by 2000, 89m. It followed on his figures (not undisputed, but less disputed than similar exercises in the past) that a third airport was necessary.

But where? This ground has been well tilled. The small airport at Stansted was earmarked for development in the mid-1960s. Then the Roskill Commission reported in the early 1970s that a new site should be developed at Cubbington. That was rejected; instead, Mr Edward Heath's government planned a major new airport at Foulness, on the Essex marshes. The next Labour government scrapped that in 1974. In 1981 Mr Eyre started his work, and in 1983 plumped for Stansted again. The government accepted that advice in 1985. Stansted will be developed in two stages to an annual capacity of 15m passengers, with a hint that at a later date (and after a further inquiry) its limit will go up to 25m. It, too, will have a high-speed rail link to the centre of London. And it is close enough to the M11 motorway for all three airports to be within easy reach of each other along the M25.

While all this angst was going on in the suburbs, a fourth airport was being planned in the inner city. Well, not quite in the inner city, though its promoters would like you to think that it was. This is the Stolport – or short take-off and landing airport – that will open in 1987 in the Royal Docks, at the eastern edge of dockland. When at full capacity, this will provide flights for about 2.5m passengers a year from London to nearby continental cities. It will be linked to the City by the new Dockland Light Railway. The idea is that businessmen and women will leave their offices in the City or at Canary Wharf and be in Paris in a trice. This may be optimistic. At present, transport from Park and City to the east is pretty slow and the Royal Docks are a long way east – eight miles from Piccadilly Circus. Besides, at what point in London is it quicker, for all the hassle, to trek to Heathrow than to head east? My guess is that even after the completion of the Dockland Light Railway, that point will still be no further east than Piccadilly Circus. Moreover, some industry analysts say that people dashing off to Paris don't start their journeys from their offices. They start, instead, from their suburban homes, and those homes may be much closer to Heathrow or Gatwick than to the Royal Docks.

One footnote to this risky-looking venture. Though the Stolport is a minnow compared to the three main airports, those who live close to its site objected to it every bit as strongly as those who lived close to the others. Yet the scheme will be completed only four years after it was first mooted, while the investment at Stansted will have had an effective lead-time of over 30 years. Cynics would say that the reason is that those who complained about Stolport came from working-class areas of east London, without the skills of presentation that their suburban cousins were able to buy. That is only part of the story. More important is that the Royals are in the dockland development area. That has a special planning regime that concertinas the process of seeking permission for development into a few months. The speed with which Stolport has been developed will not have gone unnoticed by the British Airports Authority. Not content with getting their way over Stansted, they are already working on their next shopping list, which includes a major heliport in central London to replace the inadequate facilities at Battersea. If the Airports Authority believes that speed is of the essence, dockland can expect that benefit – if such it is – as well.

The people's Cadillac

Consider some remarkable statistics. In the United Kingdom as a whole, only 2% of all journeys are made by rail. In London, 7% of journeys are on trains, and in inner London 8%. In 1854, 80% of all workers in the City arrived at their places of employment on foot; a century later, 90% travelled by public transport. If homes *versus* roads has been one of the dominant political questions facing London for the last two decades, its public transport system has exercised the minds of Londoners for nearly two centuries.

Only those Londoners who never visit any other of the world's great cities could say that the system is anything other than tremendous, though there is of course room for improvement in its coverage, costs and standards of service. If you count hackney carriages and sedan chairs, there has been a public transport of sorts in London since the seventeenth century. The sedan chairs' present-day equivalent is the London cab, of which there are now about 13,000 licensed to pick up passengers on the street, and untold numbers of minicabs, for which you have to telephone.

Despite the tendency among visitors to London to get starry-eyed about cabs and cabbies, my guess is that they are no longer loved by Londoners as they once were. Their reputation originally rested on three factors. They were not prohibitively expensive; they were as fast as the driver could make them, because he always looked for the short-cut that only his kind knew (all cab-drivers have to pass a test known as "the Knowledge", which should in theory get them familiar with all London's streets), and the cabbies themselves were great London characters.

Cabs are no longer cheap. That is partly no fault of the cabbies; London's traffic has grown so dense that the amount of time spent sitting in traffic jams with the meter ticking away grows longer by the week.

I think the traffic has bred a cynicism among cabbies. When I first came to London I learnt by heart the back routes that the best cab-drivers use to get from one place to another — who would guess how easy it is to drive from Brent Cross to Gower Street via Primrose Hill? – but I find now that few cabbies bother to use these routes at all. That does not mean that the modern cabbie is ignorant about his city, in the way in which New York taxi-drivers can be. But it does mean that too many of them seem content to sit in the main, clogged, roads.

You can, of course, still find the north London cabbie with the heart of gold, prepared to rabbit on about any subject under the sun. But you're now more likely to find a surly youth who doesn't want to talk at all, and who gets more than a little irate if you dare to suggest that he just might take a left, and then a second right, down some back street. Most of my recent conversations with cabbies have been a one-way moan in which he tells me how awful the traffic is (as if I didn't know) and how horrid his cab is; cold, noisy and smelly. New cabs have been promised for years; it is now said that they will appear in 1987.

For those not able to afford a cab, some form of transport which carries more than a few people is essential, as it has been since the late eighteenth century. That was when stage coaches, used mainly for carrying mail to outlying parts of the country, started to carry passengers on shorter stages within London. By 1800, regular services from London to nearby towns like Greenwich and Croydon had started, and 1829 saw the first inner-city omnibus service, from Paddington to the Bank of England. Over 6,000 buses now ply the streets of the capital for business. Like the tubes, they are under the control of London Regional Transport (LRT), which has a board of members appointed by the Secretary of State for Transport, and is subject to direction from him.

LRT is a recent creation; it has only had responsibility for public transport in London since 1984. Until 1933, both buses and tubes were run by private enterprise. The largest bus venture was the London General Omnibus Company, but throughout the 1920s hundreds of "pirate" buses competed with those of the "General" for custom; sometimes two buses would screech to a halt at the same queue of passengers. Few of the bus companies were hugely profitable; nor, apparently, were the privately financed underground railways (whose history we shall look at below). These, since 1907, had shared a common logo; the Chairman of the UndergrounD (sic) was Lord Ashfield, one of London's unsung heroes. In 1929 the Underground and the General decided to co-ordinate their services. That was the same year that Herbert Morrison, London's leading Labour Party politician, became Minister of Transport. He worked with Ashfield to rationalise and extend the system, and in 1933 the London Passenger Transport Board – in effect, Britain's first nationalised industry – was set up. It was superseded by the London Transport Executive in 1948, and that was placed under the control of the new GLC in 1965. By this time conventional wisdom had it that London Transport's golden age had passed, as the charms of tubes and buses were overtaken by the flexibility of the motor-car.

All was changed utterly when the Labour Party won the GLC elections in 1981. Its platform included a massive reduction in fares through increased revenue subsidy for London Transport from the GLC – or rather, from the ratepayers. This enraged the Tory-controlled borough of Bromley. Ashfield and Morrison had never taken into their system the surface railways in south London, which in 1948 passed to the newly nationalised British Railways (now British Rail, or BR). So a borough like Bromley had plenty of buses, but no tubes at all. Its councillors felt that they were being forced to ask their ratepayers to chip in for the benefit of other Londoners, and took the GLC to court. After many alarums and excursions, Bromley won. Appalled at the chaos, the government quickly prepared a bill to do away with the GLC's control over public transport, and set up the LRT under its own wing. That now has two operating arms; one for buses and one for tubes.

The buses are of more importance for trips across London than for ones that follow the radial, spokes-of-a-wheel pattern; they fill in the gaps between railways. The average length of a bus journey is just over two miles, much shorter than the five-mile average tube journey. Though there are some routes in central London where a bus is much more convenient than a tube (for example, from Piccadilly to Battersea) their main significance is in the suburbs. It follows from these characteristics that buses are used proportionately more for shopping, and less for journeys to work, than the tube: 30% of all bus trips are for shopping, but only 11% of tube trips; 35% of bus trips take people to and from work, compared with 58% of tube trips. These figures significantly affect the nature of the respective bus and tube clienteles. Buses always feel much more the working-class form of transport, full of ladies going about their shopping always ready to tell you where your best stop is. My mother-in-law travels round London by bus just for a good natter. You don't get that on the tube; people sit in silence, buried in their papers, or, increasingly during the rush hour, in a book. Tubes attract crazies and weirdos, and sometimes criminals. In 1984 a gang of kids armed with knives systematically went through the pockets of passengers in a tube carriage returning from the Notting Hill carnival.

But will the niceness of the buses survive OPO? That stands for one-person operation. On an OPO bus, you have to pay the driver as you enter; there is no conductor. There is little doubt that as an efficiency measure this serves the purposes of an increasingly cost-conscious LRT well. It will not suit all passengers, who may worry, too, about another LRT scheme. This is to put certain routes out to competitive tender, accepting bids both from their own workforce and other operators. At its best, that will bring down prices, too; at its worst, it will mean the rebirth of the "pirate" bus operators, with the danger that safety margins will be cut.

LRT is perfectly aware that people like the buses, and that some at least find the tubes threatening. The first underground railway – the Metropolitan – was opened in 1863 between Paddington and Farringdon Street. *The Times* thundered that it was "an insult to common sense to suppose that people would ever prefer to be driven amid palpable darkness through the foul subsoil of London". Not for the first or last time, *The Times* was wrong. According to *The London Encyclopaedia,* by 1864 no fewer than 259 proposals for railways in and around London were on the cards.

That first line was constructed by the cut-and-cover method. The line runs in a trench just below the surface, so that you have to walk down only a few steps to your train. The Metropolitan, District and Circle lines are built like this. Real connoisseurs of the tube's natural claustrophobia draw a rigid distinction between the

cut-and-cover lines – genuine underground railways –
and the tubes. The tubes are much deeper, you have to
take an escalator (which some people find scary) or a lift
(which others do) to get to the tracks. The tubes
themselves are just that; narrow smoky tunnels in which
you do not want to be stuck, but often are. These lines
were only able to be built once the tunnelling shield was
perfected in the 1890s; it was first used for the Northern
line (the "misery line", north Brookstowners call it) by
Charles Tyson Yerkes, an American who, with Ashfield,
was one of the two fathers of London's public transport.
He used the shield to build the Bakerloo and Piccadilly
lines in the years before the First World War. The Central
line, known as the "twopenny tube", had opened in 1900;
it is another deep line. Apart from extensions of the
underground lines onto the surface (of LRT's 260 miles of
railway, only 101 miles are underground) the next
milestone was the Victoria line, which speeded up the
gentrification of Islington when it opened in 1968. The
Victoria line runs from the north-east of your tube map to
the south-west. A further line, the Fleet, was planned to
run in the opposite direction, into the heart of Crescent,
both north and south of the river. Public expenditure cuts
in the 1970s meant that it has so far only been built as far
as Charing Cross. It was opened in 1977, by which time,
in commemoration of the great events of that year, it had
been renamed the Jubilee line.

For those into trivia, the tube network has 247 stations,
272 escalators and nearly 4,000 railway cars. This
network now handles over 670m journeys a year, or
3,340m passenger miles. The buses, by contrast, handle
1,160m journeys a year, but only 2,620m passenger miles.
OPO is being adopted on the older lines; modern ones
like the Victoria and Jubilee are damn-near automatic.
OPO on the tubes? Well, everyone says it's fine and
dandy, but it still gives people who are scared witless in
the deep lines a touch of the horrors.

OPO, on both buses and tubes, should be seen in the

light of LRT's general effort to bring down the costs of its
£1 billion-a-year operation. It has, for example, made a
determined effort to cut overmanning. Total staff
numbers have fallen from over 60,000 in 1979 to about
53,000 now, and it is LRT's firm intention to get them
lower still – a target of about 43,000 is what I suspect they
have in mind. Put that together with its tendering policy
on the buses, with the new Travelcards which enable you
to go anywhere in an LRT zone, on bus or tube, for a flat
fee (about 800,000 people now use these) and with much
better marketing, and LRT is approaching the position
that only Hong Kong of all the world's large mass transit
systems has – the ability to pay its way without relying on
subventions from the public purse. Or, at least, without
relying on such subventions for its running costs. Even
the most optimistic of LRT's management doubt whether
it will ever be able to generate enough surplus to finance
its capital needs for new buses and trains — and LRT
spends about £200m a year on its capital account.

   One of the most heartening aspects of the new
management at LRT has been its determination to work
with BR, which controls both the London suburban rail
network and most of the lines south of the river.
Surprisingly, it is only in the last few years that serious
efforts have been made to integrate the two networks, and
there is still much to be done. Many interchanges
between LRT and BR lines are still less than satisfactory.
Although there is now one map that shows all London's
railway lines, it is not set out in a way which makes the
contribution of BR's lines clear. The GLC was keen to take
over some of BR's under-used lines and give them to
London Transport (as it then was). The LRT is unlikely to
go that far, though it may in future run its own trains on
more BR lines south of the river. That will be a relief to
many of BR's customers. Trouble with both trade unions
and with the government, which has starved it of capital
for years, means that many commuters from Waterside
and Downland still have to travel up to town in BR rolling

stock fit only for the knacker's yard – cold and smelly,
with more graffiti and general untidiness than you see on
most LRT trains. BR, too, has long seemed unsure about
whether it really wanted people to travel on some of its
most useful lines, like the north London route that goes
from Richmond to the City. Slowly, that position seems to
be changing; BR is cleaning up its stations and there now
seems much more of a willingness by both operators to
work together for the good of the travelling public. In
1986 BR announced that it was to examine whether all its
commuter lines might not be given a new corporate
identity, and a new commercial freedom to go with it.

One aspect of the new mood has been the construction
of the Dockland Light Railway from the Tower into the
docklands development area. This is projected to go as far
as the Stolport, with a northern spur up to Hackney and a
southern one down into the Isle of Dogs. As part of the
package that will fund the massive financial services
centre in Canary Wharf, private developers now intend
that the Light Railway should be continued underground
from the Tower to Bank, thus providing a continuous link
from the heart of the old financial district to what may
turn out to be the new one.

Two better than four

No discussion of transport in London would be complete
without a mention of those who use two legs or two
wheels. Walking is one of the main methods used for
getting around central London and is often delightful,
though there are only a few pedestrianised streets.
Motorcyclists have come into their own in the last
decade, with the boom of despatch rider firms (how did
we ever cope without them?). Young daredevils race their
bikes to deliver packages all over town, travelling at
breakneck speeds. Many tut-tut at the noise and smell of
this. I disagree. For me, the kids on the motorbikes are an
almost romantic throwback to Paul Revere or the men

who carried the message from Ghent to Aix and
Thermopylae to Athens.

By common consent, bicycle travel is much more
civilised. It should be used much more than it is; large
parts of both west and south London are as flat as a
pancake. Some routes are indeed popular – the trip from
the Fulham Road through South Kensington to Sloane
Square and the West End is full of bikes most mornings.
But the potential for the use of bikes in London will not
be met as long as cycling is so dangerous. I bike all over
London; like every cyclist I know, I have had more
accidents than I can remember, including one spill, in
broad daylight on Kensington High Street, that wrote off
my bike and came perilously close to writing off me. The
answer is far more cycle lanes. London has been
scandalously slow to introduce these. It is only a few
years since some cycle track was dedicated through Hyde
Park, and the Royal Park Police, who appear to have
nothing better to do, still wait behind trees ready to
pounce on you if you stray from it. In this respect, the
passing of the GLC will be a big loss. Cyclists were part of
Livingstone's rainbow coalition; his administration
proposed a bike network of 1,000 miles through London.
It is now most unlikely that that will be built. So every
day we continue to take our lives in our hands. Still, for
all its perils, I wouldn't give up my bike for the world.
Better by far the dangers of that than the frustration of
London's tailbacks.

5
WORK: DOWNBEAT

Nearly 3.5m people work in London, in as wide a spread
of occupations as could be found in any city in the world.
Some are among the most highly paid in Europe, some
among the most skilled. Others live on the breadline,
eking out a living without the protection of trade unions,
minimum wage laws or social security. Some make
millions from a visit to their Lloyd's underwriters once a
week; others are illegal immigrants, working all the hours
that Allah sends in some miserable Shoreditch sweat-
shop. Some, newly arrived from western Ireland, live in
miserable digs, hang around Camden Station at 5 o'clock
every morning waiting for a start, and work on rickety
scaffolding with no national insurance to protect them if
they fall. Others swan in from the Chilterns in a
Rolls-Royce and swan out again to tax-break health
hydros, to be pampered and pummelled for the good of
their firm.

And it was ever thus. For the contrasts that make
London such a fascinating city have been all around the
acute observer for years. Indeed, there is little chance of
understanding the London economy of today unless one
understands the London economy of a century ago. In
1880, London was the greatest commercial centre the
world had ever known. All kinds of service industries
had developed on the back of the City's position as
financier and lawyer to an empire. The prosperity of
London led to an explosion of retailing and a growth of
domestic services. Many of those quite modest terraced
houses in Brookstown were built with a small room at the
top, often with a plain door and smaller windows than
elsewhere in the house (this book has been written in one

such room). They were for servants. As the terraces spread outwards, so the transport industry grew, to take those who lived in the suburbs into their shops and offices.

A three-legged chair

At the same time as London's commercial success bred a shoal of service industries to meet the needs of the middle-class who worked in it, so the port provided a second prop to the economy. London was one of the main nineteenth-century gateways for both Britain and Europe. The port provided jobs in stevedoring, in packaging, in distribution (there was, until quite recently, a whole industry that shipped and trans-shipped goods by water) and in the "finishing" trades. These latter took the raw materials that came from America or the Empire – wood, leather, foodstuffs, jewels, metal and fibres – and turned them into furniture, clothes, processed food, fittings and craftwork. For every one job in the nineteenth-century docks, there were three in dock-related industries. Hardwood came into the East India Dock, and thence, after the opening of the Regent's Canal in 1820, went to be cut, planed and turned at Shoreditch. Food followed the river too; the processing industry was centred first around the Surrey Docks, but soon had offshoots as far west as Battersea and Fulham. Tate & Lyle's sugar refinery on the banks of the river at Silvertown is, to this day, one of the largest single employers of labour in London.

As the city grew, so did the demands of those who lived in it for efficient public services like public health protection, education and housing. From 1911 onwards, central government expanded its activities; the great ministries in Whitehall filled up with clerks, secretaries and mandarins. Thus public administration had already become, by the turn of the century, the third of the three legs which supported London's economy.

This London of a century ago was a rich city; probably, in terms of its output per head, the richest in the world. (London remains richer in this sense than any other part of Britain; every category of its workforce is, on average, better paid than that of any other of Britain's regions.) Yet on the margins of this wealth was great poverty. The poverty was there for two reasons. The first was the displacement of families by the railway boom and slum clearance. The second was the extent of casual labour, which guaranteed breadwinners a job and income only for a few days a week, or at certain times of the year. Dockwork was the leader of the casual trades and continued its casual nature until the 1960s. Other jobs were more specifically seasonal; the gasworks, for example, provided employment for far more people in the winter than in the summer. Some trades depended on the erratic supply of commodities from abroad. If trade slumped, if the commodities failed to come in, if fashions changed, these casual workers had no guarantee of anything like continuous employment. The middle-classes knew all about casualisation and its attendant poverty, and about the hundreds of thousands who were, almost literally, outcasts in London. There were riots during the slump of the 1880s; the "mob" moved into the city centre; the rich and powerful were abused in their carriages.

The golden years
As we saw in Chapter 3, the housing associations were one manifestation of the self-interested altruism that developed to head off the problem of outcast London. But two other, related, social phenomena did more to share London's prosperity among all its people. The first was the growth of trade unionism; a series of strikes before the First World War finally established the power of organised labour in the port and port-related business. The second was the growth of manufacturing industry.

Until the inter-war years, manufacturing was a comparatively unimportant component of the London economy. The great factories and mills of the nineteenth century had gone to the coalfields of the Midlands or North; industries like ship-building and heavy engineering congregated where there was cheap power and easy access to iron ore. London had never had anything like cotton mills or coal mines; it had never had single businesses employing thousands of workers. Like much else, that picture did not survive the First World War. Munition, vehicle and airframe factories were attracted by the huge pools of labour that only London could provide. Once planted, a manufacturing tradition quickly took root. On some estimates a remarkable 80% of all new manufacturing plant built between the wars was in or around London; about 66% of all new jobs in the 1930s were there. The inter-war years – just the time when most of Britain was going through a slump – were London's boom times.

Apart from the pools of labour that the First World War factories had tapped, there were three main reasons for the growth of manufacturing. The first was the availability of space on which new factories could be built. Some of these estates can still be seen, at Wembley, for instance, or along the Great West Road. The second was the creation of tariff walls around new products like motor-cars and 'planes. Imports of cars between the wars, for example, were always much less than 10% of the total home market. Thus companies like Ford at Dagenham, or the tyre factories along the Great West Road, were essentially insulated from much of the world recession. Thirdly, with the coming of the national electricity grid in the early 1930s, London had its own source of power; the coal-rich areas of Scotland, the Midlands and the North lost the one comparative advantage they had over the capital.

Park Royal Estate at the southern edge of Metroland exemplifies these changes better than any other place in

London. By 1914 there were already companies on the site making car components. During the First World War, 120 acres were given over to munitions and aircraft components; then in 1925, Heinz arrived with a massive food-processing plant. That spawned other businesses like packaging. Heavy engineering came too; the estate had car factories owned by Sunbeam and Standard, and the main factory for London Transport's buses. In 1935, the Guinness brewery opened, and became the biggest employer on the site. Park Royal had everything; space, a pool of labour on its doorstep, a protected home market for some of its main products, electricity, and easy access to railways. Into its production lines, and to those of Ford, Hoover, and a host of other companies (note how many of the ones we have named were American) trooped the hordes of outcast London, to be employed in factories built like palaces, at pay levels protected by their trade unions.

It is not surprising that many of those who have the interests of London at heart should look back on those years as a golden age, and try to recreate it. It is not simply the scale of new employment during the inter-war years that is significant. As important was the dignity which that labour was given, and the extent to which the manufacturing boom removed the spectre of casualisation and poverty from a large section of London's workforce. That the golden age of the factories is over is beyond dispute. At its height, Park Royal employed nearly 50,000 people; it now has only about half that. Hoover's Perivale plant is no longer used for manufacturing; Ford once employed nearly 30,000 workers in London, now only about 16,000. In 1951, there were more than 1.5m people employed in manufacturing in London. Within the next year, that figure will almost certainly dip below 500,000, or about one person in seven of London's workforce.

Killing the goose
Two quite distinct questions need to be asked about the

collapse of London's manufacturing industry. The first is
"why did it happen"? The second – much more difficult –
is "does it matter"? In one sense, of course it matters if a
significant sector of the economy disappears. Even if the
factories relocated outside London, there would still be
transitional economic costs, and much personal misery,
caused by the scale of uprooting that took place. Yet the
question needs asking all the same. For the manufacturing years may have been golden only in a certain sense. It
may, instead, pay to look at them as no more than a little
blip in London's 2,000 year history – a few years when
technology made factories and London look as if they
were natural bedfellows rather than nodding acquaint-
ances. If that view is right, then the consequences of the
flight of manufacturing might be less awful than is
commonly supposed. London's job, in this view, would
be to re-establish an economy based on those elements of
its three traditional supports which are still in place,
while taking the opportunities that make it the natural
location for many new businesses.

There is, indeed, some evidence that the importance of
manufacturing has been overplayed. In 1977, for
example, (a year chosen deliberately – it is before the
great shake-out of manufacturing jobs that the British
economy suffered in 1979-81), only one of London's top
ten private-sector employers, Ford, was in heavy
industry. One other, Thorn EMI, was mainly in light
engineering. Of the other eight, three – Sainsbury's,
Marks & Spencer and the London Co-operative Society,
were retailers. The big four banks were there, and so was
Mirror Group Newspapers. Only Ford had as many as
30,000 employees. Yet in the same year, London's local
authorities had nearly 250,000 employees, the central
government civil service 100,000, the GLC and Inner
London Education Authority 95,000 between them,
London Transport 56,000, the National Health Service
45,000, while the Post Office, British Rail, British
Airways and the Metropolitan Police all employed more

workers than Ford. In other words, London is not a town of large, private-sector, manufacturing companies, and apart from a few years between the wars, it never has been.

None of this is to imply that the decline of manufacturing was either a natural good – after all, the more broadly based an economy is, the more likely it is to withstand trauma – or inevitable. In large measure the decline of manufacturing was willed; it did not just happen by act of God.

To understand why, it is essential to remember that the golden years were golden only for London. Outside the metropolis, Britain was in a slump. Many commentators and politicians looked at the prosperity and sheer size of London and concluded that it had grabbed too many of the goodies. To this sense of unfairness were added two other considerations. First, as war became more likely, the concentration of new industry around London began to look strategically less than wise. Early projections of the devastation that bombing would cause in London were staggering. Secondly, the sprawl of London since 1918, in which London Transport, manufacturers and builders had all colluded, gave rise to the first stirrings of "green" politics. As industry and housing spread in ribbon developments along the radial arteries, as billboards lined roads deep into the countryside, so the first generation of conservationists began to argue that London's growth must be constrained. In 1937 the Royal Commission on the Distribution of the Industrial Population (the "Barlow Commission") started to see how that goal might be achieved.

Barlow reported in 1940, just when it was reasonable to hope that planning production, manpower and land use might contribute to victory. If the war could be planned, might not the peace also? It is in that context that one should view both Barlow and other reports to the wartime government on the future of London. Barlow believed in the dispersal of industry, and argued that "the scheme of the Garden City is the model towards which the location of industry should work". But Sir Patrick Abercrombie, a member of the Commission, wanted to go much further. In a minority report, he urged the establishment of a new ministry to have the power to control the location of industry. He was then appointed, first by the London County Council and then by the government, to submit two reports on London. Unsurprisingly, given his own position, he found it overcrowded and overpopulated, believed that it had more than its share of the nation's industry, and thought that too much of that industry existed cheek-by-jowl with housing. In a memorable phrase, he spoke of the concentration of industry in the London area causing "the expansion of the metropolis to a size that is quite unmanageable and one which has made of Londoners a race of straphangers".

His solution, accepted by both the wartime government and its Labour successor, was a scattering of industry out of London. New jobs would go to sites beyond a green belt. This would circle the city and protect the surrounding country from London's expansion. Outside London would be eight satellite towns – quickly called "New Towns" – where Londoners and their jobs would go. To quote Abercrombie once more: "A number of authorities in East London could combine to form a new East or West Ham in one of the Essex satellites. A certain measure of the old community life would be transferred, the old and familiar faces of neighbours and friends would still be there."

Given how hard the first 20 years of the New Towns turned out to be, and given how much old communities protested at the uprooting forced upon them (to say nothing of the protests of the indigenous population of the New Towns at an influx of Londoners), it would be easy to mock. Certainly, it would be absurd to blame either the Barlow Commission or Abercrombie's elegant vision for London's subsequent ills. Nonetheless, it is fair to point out two failings in these reports. First, both the

New Town concept and the idea of a green belt were essentially nineteenth-century ideas, developed from Ebenezer Howard's belief in the moral rectitude of garden cities. To put it at its most mild, these ideas had not been shown to be appropriate for a twentieth century where ordinary people were both more prosperous and more mobile than Howard could ever have imagined. Planning that people and their jobs should be in one place rather than another is fine when individuals do not have the resources to make those choices for themselves. When they do, such plans are apt to go awry.

Secondly, in some key respects, the data that both the Barlow Commission and Abercrombie used was almost certainly out of date. It now seems tolerably clear that by the late 1930s, and without any government encouragment, the population of London was already dropping quite sharply. Moreover, there is now some evidence that by the same time the boom in London's manufacturing was over. New businesses already found London crowded and its costs high. In other words, left to themselves, market forces would almost certainly have solved the problems that so worried Abercrombie and successive governments.

Nonetheless, the New Towns were built. Stevenage was the first; Hemel Hempstead, Harlow, Bracknell, Basildon, Hatfield, Welwyn Garden City and Crawley followed. Not all firms would, of their own free will, have moved to the New Towns. The official history of the LCC puts the point with a delicacy worthy of Orwell: "Considerable efforts of persuasion were needed. Direct approaches were made to firms whose premises were situated in areas zoned for other purposes in the Plan. A sum of money was allocated for the purchase of such premises. This often facilitated the movement of an industry." Quite.

The policy of decentralisation of industry was not limited to encouraging growth in the New Towns. Throughout the 1950s and 1960s the successive governments followed a "regional policy" which gave cost advantages to firms who wanted to settle in the old depressed regions of the North, Wales or Scotland. This exacerbated the pattern of decisions that firms were already taking for themselves. Despite the bombing, by the 1950s there were few green-field sites available in London, especially as the technology of manufacturing demanded large expanses of floorspace. Both rates and rents have always been higher in London than elsewhere. So have wages, but as a factor encouraging the flight of manufacturing they are probably of less importance, for the productivity of London's workforce has usually been higher than that in the rest of Britain.

Luddism and lack of imagination

Sometimes, as in the furniture industry, which employed 60,000 workers in London in 1951, but only 12,000 in 1984, the job loss can only be explained by a failure of British manufacturers to adapt to new technology and marketing systems as successfully as their continental competitors. In other sectors, that failure on the part of management was not helped by the defensiveness of trade unions. London has been a "union town" since the first part of this century. Without question, that has brought benefits to much of the workforce. Unionisation, and the coming of multinationals after 1918, were two important reasons for the disappearance of outcast London. But there is a downside to the power in London of trade unions. The printing industry, for example, which now employs more people than any other manufacturing sector, has perhaps lost opportunities to be even bigger by a failure to adapt to new technology. This has been particularly marked on Fleet Street, where the national newspapers have traditionally been written and printed.

In principle, newspapers should be a highly profitable business. The British have an insatiable appetite for newsprint, and computer typesetting provides the opportunity to reduce the cost of producing those papers.

In fact, most British newspapers are anything but money-making. That is mainly because successive managements have looked on the business as a toy, and have given up the right to recruit labour and organise work to the strong craft-based print unions. That gives Fleet Street a unique feel, with its workers (almost all male, almost all white) representing a fly-by-night aristocracy of labour. Until very recently, overmanning was so bad that some people were paid to do jobs not even needed for old hot-metal printing technology. In the view of one analyst of Fleet Street, it would make more sense for national newspapers to fund the minicab firms of east London directly rather than pay their typesetters such large wages for such little work that they can moonlight on the side.

This most odd of all London's industrial worlds, stuck between the City and the West End, is changing rapidly. But in a tragically British way, it is changing only under pressure, and in the short term yet more jobs will be lost. The catalyst for the present drama in Fleet Street is Eddie Shah, a young businessman who made his money producing free newspapers in the north of England. Having weathered a strike by the print unions in 1984, he decided that he could use new technology to launch a national daily. Such a paper, typeset directly onto computer by its journalists, would break down the traditional job demarcations between the different crafts in the printing trade and between printers and journalists. It would cut costs all round, and Shah found that he could get his overheads even lower by setting up in Pimlico rather than Fleet Street, and by breaking out of the accepted distribution pattern for newspapers. His paper *Today* hit the streets in March, 1986. It employs only 600 people; that is 10% of the number that the Mirror Group employed pre-Shah.

Pre-Shah, but not post-Shah. For in one sense, fast Eddie did no more than persuade the other companies to do what they knew was sensible all along. The Mirror

Group, now owned by Robert Maxwell, *The Guardian*
(independently owned), the Telegraph group (family-
owned until a financial crisis in 1985 led to its takeover
by Canadian Conrad Black – one of those wild colonial
boys who have always had an eye on British newspapers),
and News International, publisher of four titles and run
by Rupert Murdoch, once an Australian, now an
American, had all long planned moves from the cramped
confines of Fleet Street to the new frontier of dockland.
The question was, how could they make the assets in
which they had invested so much (in *The Daily* and
Sunday Telegraph's case, enough to bankrupt the group)
sweat a bit of cash? Shah encouraged them to be bold.

The first move was made by Maxwell, who in January
1986 negotiated a cut in manning and new agreements
with the print unions, the NGA and SOGAT '82. That
approach did not suit Murdoch. Whether he wanted to
break the power of the unions once and for all, or whether
he felt that they could not deliver a sufficient reduction in
costs, is not clear. His tactics, though, were both clear and
dramatic. Having failed to convince the print unions to
sign a new deal of which the two key elements were a cut
in manning levels and a declaration of management's
right to manage (exactly, in other words, what the old
proprietors had been willing to concede) Murdoch closed
his central London plants and moved *The Times, The
Sunday Times,* the *News of the World* and *The Sun* to
Wapping overnight, sacking 5,000 print workers as he did
so.

He was able to get away with this largely because other
trade unions had had enough of watching the print
workers first build their gravy train and then eat, sleep
and drink on it. With the help of the electricians' union,
EETPU, Murdoch was able to recruit enough newcomers
to the industry to staff his new plant. After much angst,
and under a lot of pressure, the bulk of News
International's journalists followed suit, unprepared,
when the chips were down, to show solidarity with their

brothers in the print shop. At the time of writing it is much too early to predict the outcome of this war. With luck, when the battle is over, new titles will be legion, and new jobs for printers and journalists will have been found. But that blissful day has not yet dawned. For the moment, the print industry is just another of those examples where the British wake up too late to the possibilities of a new market and new technology, panic, and watch in horror as jobs are lost.

The decline of jobs in dockland has some of the same sad elements seen in the printing trade. The first enclosed dock built in London was the West India Dock on the Isle of Dogs, in 1802. Throughout the nineteenth century, private capitalists financed other docks. The magnificent culmination of the building boom was the Royal Dock complex, way to the east, between Plaistow and the river. The Royal Victoria was opened in 1855, the Royal Albert (the biggest of them all, nearly a mile long with three miles of wharves) in 1880 and the King George V in 1921. The King George was the last upstream dock to be built; by the time it was opened, the docks had for 13 years been owned publicly, through the Port of London Authority (PLA). Competition for the river trade had not proved profitable.

Nor, soon, did the monopoly of the PLA. Like the rest of London's economy, the port had golden days in the 1930s, when Silvertown Way was known as the Road to the Empire, and all but the very biggest Cunard liners could dock in the Royals. Like the rest of London's economy, those days did not survive the 1950s. A lack of investment in new facilities, when competitor ports like Rotterdam were doing all they could to attract trade, was one factor. So was the preference of shippers for ports closer to the mouth of the Thames or off the tideway altogether. Most crucial, however, was the coming of containerisation and trade union reaction to it.

The docks, remember, had been the prime example of casual labour. Dockers' jobs were protected from 1947, and finally decasualised in 1967. But the job protection heaped enormous costs on the PLA. Because it had to absorb those made redundant from private firms on the river, while it was unable to sack any of its workers, its total workforce grew during the 1950s and 1960s, at the time when it should have been shrinking. For the coming of containerisation changed the whole nature of dockwork; once most sea-going freight could be carried in containers, shippers started looking for sites where the stuffing and stripping of containers could be done without some of the costs and old facilities of the upstream docks. Tilbury, way down the northern bank of the river, and Felixstowe, on the North Sea, were the favoured locations. Thus between 1967 and 1981, when the Royals finally closed, dock employment shrank by 20,000. And as the economy of east London was so tied to trade in the docks, other jobs went too; about 50,000 in manufacturing (mainly in the finishing trades like food-processing and furniture manufacture), 10,000 in construction, and 30,000 in inland transport.

The devastation wrought on east London was appalling. I can remember walking through the Isle of Dogs in 1980 and finding it the most silent place I could ever imagine. The cranes, one felt, were rusting before one's eyes; the very water looked stagnant. Along Wapping High Street, where the gentrifiers had not yet moved in, huge warehouses formed canyons on either side of the street, deserted all; behind them a wall of old LCC flats dripped in the damp. Even Hawksmoor's masterpiece, St. George-in-the-East, could lighten little of the gloom.

Yet it will not do to be sentimental about the decline of dockland. There was a nasty side to it; the white, male, macho worker at his worst. Pubs with knock-off goods; the decamping of the Chinese community in Limehouse after 1945 to make way for "our people"; the dockers who marched on the West End to support Enoch Powell's racism (you wouldn't see many blacks or women in old Fleet Street either) – all these were as much a part of the fabric of east London as the camaraderie of the Blitz and Coronation Day street parties. (The racism is still there; some estates in Tower Hamlets and Newham are no-go areas for Asians, many of whom have had to weather the most appalling treatment from East End racist thugs). The dark side of east London life is one reason why attempts to remake it in its old image are not just unrealistic but also undesirable. Dockland is now a test bed of the whole of London – perhaps even for the whole British economy. Can a depressed inner-city area, whose principle economic activity has departed, build a new life from non-traditional businesses?

Shops and offices

Most of the gloom surrounding London's economy centres on the decline of manufacturing. That leads some to assume that the service sector must have had things all its own way for the last 20 years. Not so. Take retailing. Though Park and City – especially the old West End and Knightsbridge – have become one of the world's great retail centres, other parts of the city have seen their shops disappear. In the last ten years, 10,000 shops have closed in London, including 2,000 neighbourhood food shops. In the 1979-81 shakeout, 29,000 jobs were lost in retailing.

As usual in London, this decline of economic activity did not take place with equal effect all over the city. The Crescent was worst hit, for two reasons. First, more shops closed there, leaving the neighbourhood shopping streets run-down and flyblown. Take as an example Tottenham High Road, which quite recently was a thriving shopping centre but which is now just one boarded-up front after another. Southwark, Tower Hamlets and Hackney are full of streets in a similar state.

The second reason for the unequal impact of retail decline is the pattern of new shop-building. Tesco and Sainsbury's now move no less than 55% of all packaged groceries in London and, though they will often have shops in poorer areas, their new superstores will tend to be where their customers have money, or where they can drive to the shop, or both. In no case does that mean the Crescent. Of the 50 "superstores" (supermarkets with more than 20,000 square feet of shelf space) built or under construction in London, 75% are in the outer city. As they start up, so shops closer in are shut down.

The drift of the big shops to London's periphery will increase. The retailers were among the first to identify the strategic potential of the M25. Those who live close to the orbital motorway can afford cars; that means that they are reasonably well off, and that the retailer can build on a green-field site, with easy access for "just in time" deliveries. Good news all round; but bad news for those left in the inner city, with a declining number of shops, a declining choice of goods in those shops that are left, and no cars to escape to the cheap superstores.

Office employment, too, has not been all roses. It has suffered from the same planning catastrophes that dogged manufacturing. Start with the LCC plan of 1960, which brooked no argument. "Despite steps taken to restrain the expansion of offices in central London", it said, "office employment has continued to increase." The whole point of the plan was to decrease it. Office employment rose by 63% in the 20 years to 1951, and most of that growth was in the office blocks of Park and City. By the late 1950s that central area had a quarter of all of Britain's office workers. That was too much for the LCC. Worried by the strap-hanger image, and convinced that the centre of town might grind to a halt if commuting was not reduced, the LCC adopted a decentralisation policy in 1957. Offices were discouraged in central London, and told to move to the new or expanding towns. Later, in the 1960s, this became a national policy, with the Location of Offices Bureau working like mad to send offices anywhere but central London.

The civil service led the way. With many protests from

the unions, it packed its clerical workers off to Glasgow, Bootle, Newcastle, Cardiff and Sheffield. But these policies were adopted at just the wrong time. Office employment had been leaving London since the war, following its manufacturing markets out of town. Though some new service industries have done well in London in the last 20 years, London has not had nearly as fast a growth of service-sector employment as the rest of the south-east. In 1971-81, for example, the south-east outside London saw a 24% growth of service-sector employment; in London the service sector as a whole shrank. Moreover, such new jobs as there are in the capital tend to be not in Park and City. About 1m less people work in Park and City than did 20 years ago. About 1m more than then work in outer London; that is why town centres like Romford and Croydon – or even Hammersmith, with its little band of American multinationals – have shown such a growth of prosperity.

The decline in office employment in central London was not expected, and was not appreciated until the 1971 census was analysed. When the penny dropped, Londoners were already getting most upset about the number of empty office blocks in the West End – Centrepoint, at the corner of Charing Cross Road and Oxford Street, was the most notorious. The blocks were left empty for two reasons. First, property developers could get huge tax write-offs to finance their next investment. Second, the crude demand for large West End office space declined. In particular, the old-style headquarters building employing 2,000 typists was a thing of the past. Companies like BP and ICI actually started to move their headquarters out of London (ICI more successfully than BP); newcomers like IBM had representative offices in London, but headquarters elsewhere in the south-east. Though matters were no doubt complicated by its odd, thin profile, the years taken to let Centrepoint itself were some indication of the changing times. With a slow grinding of gears, the decentralisation policy began to go into reverse. For the last few years, both central and local government have been keen to attract offices to London, not scare them away.

Outcast London revisited?

Because London's population has been in constant decline since the 1930s, the loss of jobs in the capital throughout the years 1945-75 was not accompanied by substantial unemployment. Indeed, throughout those years, London had a much lower unemployment rate than the rest of the country (it is still less, though the gap has narrowed to 1-2%). But the rate of unemployment has risen much faster in London than elsewhere. Perhaps because London's manufacturing firms hung on through recession a little longer than those in other of Britain's cities, it was not until 1979-81 that the shakeout of labour in Britain began to boost London's unemployment. On the government's figures, there are now well over 400,000 registered unemployed in London; there are probably another 120,000 (mainly married women) who are seeking work and would take paid employment if it were available. That amounts, as the GLC constantly said, to one of the largest concentrations of officially unemployed people in the advanced industrial world.

This army of the workless is billeted unevenly. Unemployment rates in inner London are much higher than in outer London, and much higher in Crescent than anywhere else. In January 1985, eight parliamentary constituencies – five north of the river in Islington, Hackney and Tower Hamlets, three south of the river in Lambeth and Southwark – had unemployment rates of more than 20%. Dome pockets within those areas had rates of nearly 30%. These districts were fringed by a ring of seats in Haringey, Camden and Newham with rates just under 20%. By contrast, seven outer London parliamentary seats in Bromley, Bexley, Sutton, Kingston and Hillingdon had unemployment rates of just 5%, well under half the national average.

The jobless figures are further differentiated by race. Asian males tend to have the same job pattern as white males, and 75% of the Asian community lives in outer London. So though Asian women have some specific difficulties in the job market, location and skill-patterns mean that Asian men are employed much as white men are. Blacks, by contrast, live in inner London, and their employment pattern is quite different from whites and Asians.

These factors alone would tend to increase the chances of black workers being unemployed. And that takes no account of racial discrimination in the job market in the form of overt racism or recruiting practices (of which the print industry is a notorious example), which limit job opportunities to the friends and relatives of those already employed. Unsurprisingly, unemployment among young black males is much worse than in any other section of the workforce. In 1981 (and things have since got worse) 33% of blacks under 25 in London were unemployed, but only 12% of whites in the same age group. In inner London, 20% of all those unemployed and 25% of those aged under 25 were black. This cannot just be put down to poor educational qualifications. According to recent academic work, blacks are 60%-100% more likely to be unemployed than whites, even among similarly qualified whites and blacks.

It is findings like these – the collapse of manufacturing, the decline of the inner city, and, above all, the high rates of young black unemployment – that lead some commentators to conclude that the days of outcast London are with us once more. Moreover, they argue that those sectors of the London economy that have expanded over the last two decades – like tourism and the catering trade – offer only part-time, non-unionised casual work, just as the docks and gasworks did a century ago. They fear the creation of a permanently deprived underclass, living cheek-by-jowl with some of the most valuable property and highly paid young professionals in the world. If they are right, the prospects for London are gloomy indeed. To check if they are wrong, we have to look at the potential for new business in London.

6
WORK: UPBEAT

John Fell (not his real name) thinks of himself as a writer – albeit one who is rarely published. He settled in London in 1979 after a decade of trotting round Britain and the world doing all sorts of jobs. His father is a builder in the north, and once in London, John teamed up with some friends – one a musician, one a photographer, one an engaging entrepreneur – to form a high-quality painting and decorating business. They have gone from strength to strength. Advertising solely by word of mouth, with one friend passing them on to another, they have not been out of work for seven years. The market for gentrification is so buoyant that their order books are not infrequently full for six months. They offer a complete service from minor building work to doing up an entire house; from top-quality carpentry to all the little tricks of the painter's art (rag-rolling is popular at the moment) which individualise a Brookstown home for its upwardly mobile owners. They will work anywhere in London, though naturally spend most of their time in the terraces of the north and west and, increasingly, just south of the river. Indeed, demand for their services in Battersea and Clapham is now so high that they could probably if they wished, just concentrate on that area. When bored, they might do a job on a client's cottage in Wales, or even in France.

John is what is known in the trade as a "ghost". He pays no taxes, save for rates on the converted studio that he, his girlfriend and their son own in Chelsea. He draws no state benefits either, though he sometimes has to make use of the National Health Service. He makes no big thing of it, but prefers to make his contribution to society by donating to every charity box he sees, and by helping out those who need jobs done cheap. His clients get a marvellous job done at a price that is automatically 15% less than an orthodox builder would charge, because John doesn't charge value-added tax on his work (though he does, of course, have to pass on to his client any VAT that he pays to building suppliers). In return, John says he gets the sense of knowing that he and his group can work at their own pace, and can set up ways of doing business that don't depend on management networks. The group could easily, by now, have turned itself into a profitable, "normal", tax-paying, firm, divided between bosses and workers. None of them have ever wanted to go down that route.

In the sense of an altruistic, vaguely counter-cultural way in which they do business, John and his friends are probably not typical. Where they are typical is in working without paying taxes, in what is known as the "black economy". The building and construction trade is the most important sector of that economy. Officially, there are over 200,000 people who work in the building trades in London, of whom perhaps 45,000 are registered as unemployed. Like other sectors of London's economy, building has had a rough decade. The collapse of London's house-building programme, with public investment in new houses halving between 1973 and 1983, has thrown many workers onto the dole. One response to that recession has been an explosion of small and one-man building firms, which increased by 50% in just three years between 1979 and 1982. No less than 85% of all London's building firms now employ less than eight people. A second response, and one that masks the true level of economic activity in the trade, is the black economy.

That economy is closely tied to trends in gentrification, and those are in turn tied to the level of improvement grants that middle-class house buyers can get to do up their property. The availability of these grants, and their levels, are a matter of policy for central and local government, which means they can be subject to enormous fluctuations. Many Londoners will remember the crazy winter of 1982-83 when the government, keen to boost the economy, upped the level of grant from 75% to 90%. Skips sprouted like demented mushrooms in the streets of Brookstown, and Friday evenings saw one of the most entertaining indicators of economic activity I can ever remember. People queued in their banks to withdraw up to £1,000 in cash, dashed into taxis and hurtled home to pay off the builders, no questions asked. (My street in west London was largely undeveloped until that year – houses that were bought in 1982 for £50,000 and then done up on the back of the 90% grants now sell for £150,000).

Those same houses are the site for another important part of the black economy – domestic help. It is quite impossible to say how many Londoners employ some assistance in their homes, and how many of those ensure that all relevant National Insurance and tax regulations are complied with.

Middle-class families with two earners are more common in London than elsewhere. The preponderance of public-sector and service-industry jobs in the capital means that there are many more opportunities for women to make a career of their own. The size of mortgages with which Londoners are often saddled can make maintaining a second income almost a necessity. At one end of the market must be quite formal arrangements. Consider live-in nannies, who have spread like a winsome plague from the houses of foreigners and aristocrats to Brookstown. Most of them probably have all the right tax formalities. At the other end of the scale are hundreds of thousands of households that employ cleaning ladies for five or six hours a week, and some, in the suburbs, who employ gardeners too. I know of quite modest households that pay three separate individuals to help with domestic chores. Common sense suggests that much of this labour is a part of the black economy.

If one puts together building work and domestic labour with other sectors, like hotels and catering, where there has always been an element of black economy moonlighting, it becomes clear that the degree of economic activity in London hidden from the official figures is substantial. Some academics have estimated that in Britain as a whole the black economy accounts for something like 6% of gross domestic product; in London, that must be a very conservative estimate.

The black economy is not an unqualified good. Quite apart from the tax revenues that are lost as a result, those who work in it have to take the risk of doing without many of the protections that are offered by the welfare state. Building workers, in particular, run risks to their health and safety by working "on the black" that they would avoid if they were employed in conventional ways. What the existence of a thriving black economy does show, however, is that the gloomy nature of London's economy suggested by the official figures is not the whole story.

Gone West

Of course, the black economy alone cannot come anywhere near solving London's economic problems, and it would be foolish to pretend that it can. Any rediscovery of the giant's strength that London once possessed must be based on a realistic assessment of the attractions of the city for job- and wealth-creating businesses. In this connection, it is of vital importance to understand the nature of London's immediate hinterland, the south-east of England.

Within an arc running from the North Sea at Harwich to the English Channel west of Southampton live more than 17m people, of whom, in 1986, a little under 40% lived in

London. But as recently as 1951, of the 15m people within that arc, 53% lived in London. By the year 2000, about 18m people will live within the south-east, of whom only about 36% will live in London. Put another way, within 50 years London will have lost 1.5m people, while the rest of the south-east will have gained 4.5m.

Though the huge amount of wealth generated by the City makes London, by any standards, the richest part of Britain, the rest of the south-east runs it an ever-closer second. In terms of domestic product per head, for example, London in 1983 had a figure of £5,600, and the rest of the south-east £4,800. In terms of both population and economic activity, the south-east outside London has been Britain's most consistent growth point since 1945. In international terms (and it is vital to remember this) the area has been only moderately successful. If, as some like to claim, it is part of north-west Europe's golden triangle (including the Paris Basin, the Low Countries, and the western part of Germany) it is only hanging in there by the skin of its teeth. But in British terms it has been an unqualified success. It even has some pockets of genuine labour shortage – a sick joke in much of the rest of Britain. Crawley, for example, on the doorstep of Gatwick airport, has an unemployment rate of less than 5%, and firms there report that they cannot recruit all the skilled labour they need.

While all of the region has grown economically and in population, some parts have grown faster than others. At present, the main growth point is on the northern edge in Buckinghamshire, where Milton Keynes looks set to become the most successful, as well as the largest, of all Britain's new towns. By contrast, economic activity is less buoyant to the east. In December 1984, for example, only four of the 17 "travel-to-work areas" (TTWAs) in Kent, East Sussex and Essex had less than 10% unemployment. In West Sussex, Surrey, Bedfordshire, Buckinghamshire, Berkshire, Oxfordshire, Hertfordshire and Hampshire, only six of the 22 TTWAs had unemployment rates of more than 10%.

We saw in Chapter 5 that successive governments have tried to disperse industry from London, and this is one of the most important reasons for the growth of the south-east. But there are others. Plain old quality of life is one of them. In the south of the region, for example, the coastlines of Hampshire and West Sussex have their attractions, with delightful harbours like Chichester providing just the place for travelling executives from IBM to bring up their children. Or you could live in one of the lush stretches of the Thames Valley, or enjoy the intellectual delights and kudos of living within spitting distance of Oxford. The M4 motorway, which links London with Bristol and the West Country, has helped the west's development. If you don't mind an hour's drive in the morning, you can live in a village within ten miles of it at any point in the hundred miles from Heathrow to Bristol and work at almost any town along its route. Access to Heathrow is also attractive for those who work in international businesses to the west of London.

Less often mentioned has been the impact of the military. The sandy heathlands of Surrey and Hampshire have always been a favourite place for soldiers. The clatter of helicopters as one drives along the M3 and A303 towards Salisbury Plain can sometimes be quite unnerving. Because it is the biggest customer for high-technology goods in Britain, the army's presence, coupled with the environmental attractions of the area, has encouraged the growth of a corridor of high-tech industries along both the M3 and M4. This has given rise to genuine boom-towns like Basingstoke and Bracknell. And all this, those who have gone to live there can say, is still within easy reach of the leisure and cultural opportunities of the capital.

This process fuels another of London's predictable party conversations. Economic activity in the city, wiseacres always say, has constantly moved west. First, in the nineteenth century, the motor of London's economy was the East End; then it was the West End; then west London (remember Park Royal?) then Heathrow, and now it is the Thames Valley and the M3 and M4 corridors. And this process, you will be told, continues. Why, look at Swindon, recently a boring Wiltshire town with little but a railway engineering works (which will soon be closed) but now, as any fool can see from the M4, bursting with modern factories. Look at Bath, where the Royal Navy is the largest employer, with all the high-income, high-tech jobs that that implies. Look at Bristol, everybody's favourite British city (God knows why), and only two hours from Piccadilly. Those are the places that people now want to live and work in.

What this kind of comment ignores is that once you are as far out as, say, anywhere beyond Reading, it is the merest affectation to claim that you have anything to do with London at all. It is simply not true that thousands of Bristolians dash into the London theatres every night, or shop each Saturday at Harvey Nichols. If you really want to feel part of London, and millions are sensible enough to want just that, there is a strictly finite limit to how far out of its centre you can live.

This leads to something of a rethink of the accepted wisdom. Despite the figures that suggest that the westward drift continues, some analysts now think its great days are over. This is for two reasons, one of which is already evident. The county councils in the south-east and in the near-west country have not the slightest intention of letting their broad acres be turned into a new heartland of manufacturing industry, even if that industry was to be housed in environmentally benign factories. Secondly, the drift to the west may stop because there is now an alternative location, much closer to London, for those who want both the facilities of the capital and green-field sites – the corridor around the M25.

If this book appears to be vaguely fixated with the M25, it is for a good reason. The motorway's impact on patterns of economic activity in London and the south-east will be profound. To the west, the M25 has made the high-tech corridor out to Reading and Basingstoke even more attractive than it was five years ago. Leisure developments are planned near Heathrow, hotels at Chertsey, and a hyperstore at Denham. Surrey and Berkshire both report interest in high-tech industrial parks. To the south, there are proposals for an industrial estate at Crawley and a leisure complex at Godstone; over in Kent, the junction of the M20 and M25 at Swanley will see light industrial and hotel building. At Dartmouth, a major distribution centre with roll-on roll-off facilities is under construction. In Essex, two developers are bidding for a massive site in Thurrock, and so it goes on around the north, with towns like St Albans, Welwyn Garden City, Harlow and Hemel Hempstead all likely to be placed under severe development pressure for warehousing, retailing, distribution centres and light industry.

How welcome is this interest in sites around the M25? Some of the jobs along its borders will, one has to concede, have done nothing but relocate from central London. Thus insofar as the inner city is a problem, the M25 will not necessarily help to solve it. On the other hand, some businesses along the motorway will be genuinely new economic activity, for two reasons. First, the corridor – at least the western end of it – will have a sufficient supply of labour skilled in tomorrow's industries, and many other parts of Britain will not. Second, it will be much easier to export to Europe from the M25 than from anywhere else in Britain. Nor should it be thought that all these new jobs will be found *outside* the motorway ring. Some county councils, after all, are going to turn down a lot of planning applications. The M25 goes through the Green Belt for all but a mile of its length; counties like Surrey have already said in the strongest terms that they will resist major developments in the belt. In truth, they have little choice if they are to avoid environmental protests; much of the Surrey sector of the M25 runs through a designated area of outstanding natural beauty as well as the Green Belt itself.

Thus the most important question about the M25 is straightforward – where will the developments that are turned down by the county councils go? If, as many will have it, they go yet further down the M4 to Bath and Bristol (or, for that matter, across the Channel) then London is in trouble. But there is no need for that to happen. On the western half of the M25 corridor, outer London boroughs like Ealing, Kingston and Sutton could all take more development. (I would bet on Sutton as the fastest-growing London borough of the 1990s). To the east, Enfield, Redbridge, Waltham Forest and Barking & Dagenham might all take developments too, and this eastern sector is likely to be further aided by the gradual development of Stansted as the third airport. Stansted will not draw business to the eastern side of London on quite the scale that the aborted airport at Foulness would have done, but it will be better than nothing, and will relieve some pressure on what would otherwise be an overheated western sector.

Something to crow about

But if the counties turn down applications for businesses outside the M25, will any of those firms choose to locate not in outer boroughs like Sutton but in the city centre? That depends on the people behind billboards, which, since 1981, have sprouted all over London featuring a jaunty crow in a bowler hat. Under the ad is the logo (not one that the New Towns appreciated): "Why move to the middle of nowhere when you can move to the middle of London?" The billboards advertise dockland; more precisely, they advertise the London Dockland Development Corporation, or LDDC. In five years, this government-appointed body has become a key factor in the economic life of London.

Once it became apparent that there was little future for the upstream docks, central government and the dockland boroughs (Tower Hamlets, Southwark, Lewisham, Newham and Greenwich) had to decide what to do with them and their surrounds. This was a problem that had faced plenty of other cities in the world – Boston, Baltimore and San Francisco, for example, have all had to handle the rundown of their waterfronts – yet for many years London seemed unable to learn from foreign experience. In part, that was understandable, for London's problem was in two ways unique. First, its scale was enormous; and by this I don't mean principally the physical size of dockland. More to the point, what was historically the most populous part of the city took its social lifeblood from the docks. When they closed, more than an economy was fractured; a close-knit and substantial community was too.

Second, London's docks do not form a neat self-contained area of waterfront. They straggle along the river from Tower Bridge to Beckton for 11 miles. At their western end they abut onto the heart of the City; at the east they are most definitely in outer London. As the crow flies, the Royal Dock complex is eight miles from Piccadilly Circus. Thus it has not been easy to devise a strategy for the regeneration of dockland which could hold good for the whole area.

That said, in the last 20 years three broad approaches to east London's problems have been identified. The first was to do nothing at all. "We should have grassed them over", a very senior London local government official once said to me. His argument was that market forces had taken both jobs and people away from dockland, and that London should recognise that fact instead of moaning about it. He argued that the amount of time spent worrying about the problems of dockland would have been better spent looking after places where people really did want to live – like Shoreditch, Brent or Brixton. If property prices in dockland collapsed so that eventually business moved back there (as has happened twice in Boston), fine; if they didn't, tough.

This attitude was never taken seriously, even by those Conservative politicians who one might have thought were most wedded to free-market solutions. The myths and legends of dockland (chirpily chatting to the Queen during the Blitz, and all that) were too strong. Something had to be done. For the Labour politicians who have always run the dockland boroughs, that something was to bring back into the area as much of its traditional business as possible. That was the course taken by the boroughs' joint strategic plan in 1976. As late as 1982, a paper by the GLC (then under Labour control) argued that the particular working-class, manufacturing nature of east London should be preserved. There was said to be a continuing role for the port; the Royals should be kept open for short trips to the Low Countries and Scandinavia; office and service-sector development should be resisted. Calls were made for major public-sector investments; any suggestion that the area might be gentrified either in terms of its economy or by the people who lived there was damned as a rejection of the unique flavour of dockland.

It is easy to understand why east Londoners and their elected representatives reacted in this way. The old pattern of community life had been destroyed, and there must have been a tremendous temptation to try to recreate the past. But quite apart from whether that past really did encompass all that is brightest and best about British working-class society – which it almost certainly did not – the enterprise was doomed from the start. The upstream port was dead, and the attitudes of those same nostalgic east Londoners to technological change was one of the things that had killed it. Without the port, the prospects for large-scale manufacturing were not good.

It was in the realisation that the past could not be recreated that the Conservative government set up the LDDC, whose first chairman, Nigel Broackes, of the Trafalgar House property-to-shipping conglomerate, was just the kind of buccaneering capitalist guaranteed to annoy most east London politicians (but not all; his first deputy chairman was Bob Mellish, an old right-wing Labour ex-minister who had fallen out with the new London Labour Party). The LDDC now has responsibility for eight square miles of land which stretch on the northern bank from Tower Bridge to the Royals, and on the south bank include the Surrey Docks at Bermondsey. It receives an annual grant-in-aid from the government of over £50m. This it uses mainly to rehabilitate land, which it then sells to private-sector developers on the open market. Those developers get a set of tax advantages including relief from local rates. They invest knowing that their plans will be put into effect quickly. For the LDDC has replaced the local boroughs as the planning authority for the region, and grants permission with few of the formalities that apply outside the development area. In the Isle of Dogs, an Enterprise Zone, the planning regime is effectively non-existent, and the tax breaks even more generous.

Not everything the LDDC has done has been marvellous. The extent to which it listens to the local community is a much debated point – certainly some locals feel that they have been left out of things. It freely admits that its policy of offering new housing to local people at below market rates has not gone smoothly. There have been worrying tales of scams and shadow purchasers, which do little to improve the reputation of the LDDC with those who wish it ill. And, as we shall see below, one of its most important development decisions involves a huge gamble which, if it does not come off, will leave egg on a lot of faces. Moreover, it can be argued that the LDDC is looking after the easy bits of east London. It has very few lousy, "sink" housing estates within its borders, though there are some (including the estate where Ronan Point still stands) just outside it. The LDDC's relationship with the dockland boroughs has been rocky – though that is no fault of its own – and in each annual report its "jobs projected" tally continues to dwarf its "new jobs created" one.

These caveats notwithstanding, the LDDC has accomplished a remarkable amount in a short time; so much so that it is easy to forget how slowly things started. Nigel Broackes had scant success in persuading the private sector to invest in dockland for the first year of the LDDC. It was not really until the Isle of Dogs Enterprise Zone was up and running that developers started to take a genuine interest in the place. Four years later, some of the claims for dockland – like that it is the biggest and most successful urban renewal project in Europe – seem not at all far-fetched.

The single most important component of the LDDC's strategy has been to go for marketing-led growth rather than for growth determined by bureaucratic plans. It has used the crows and other snappy devices to push the idea that dockland offers a unique environment – a "water city", they like to say – in Europe. Its 40 miles of waterfront are ideal for housing and recreation on the doorstep of new offices, restaurants and wine bars.

Unsurprisingly, this marketing image has attracted a slightly trendy collection of service industries. Reg Ward, the Chief Executive of the LDDC, said in 1984 that he saw five industries playing a major role in the regeneration of dockland. These were the press and printing; the media (including TV, advertisers, photographers, conference and exhibition users); computer software houses; leisure, recreation and tourism; and telecommunications technology. This list has two equally important characteristics. First, only one of those businesses – printing – could conceivably be called a traditional East End trade. The difference between what the LDDC wants for the region and what the dockland boroughs wanted for it is almost total. Second, these industries are precisely the ones, with precisely the kind of people working in them, that conventional wisdom had it would always be pulled out of London to the west. Dockland, in short, stands for nothing less than an attempt to reverse a century-old pattern of industrial location in south-east England.

Will it work? The LDDC officially claims that about 6,000 new jobs have been created since 1981, and that another 30,000 are on their way. Sceptics would say, with some justification, that those figures are too small to make much of a dent in east London's unemployment. On the other hand, the speed with which the dockland scene is changing can make any projection today look dated tomorrow; its record of attracting private capital, after that slow start, has been a good one. For every £1 of public money in dockland, private investors are now putting in nearly £8. Land which five years ago cost £75,000 an acre now changes hands for close to £1m and City analysts say that demand for property remains buoyant.

In some aspects of the LDDC project, this private investment is already changing the face of dockland. The corporation has, for example, persuaded private house-builders to come back to areas they long ago despaired of. In 1981, only 5% of the housing in dockland was in owner occupation. Over 1,500 new homes have been finished, and 7,000 are in the pipeline. There is now more house-building going on in dockland than anywhere else in London. Schemes like the Butler's Wharf and Concordia Wharf warehouse conversions will end up among the most sought-after residential complexes in the city. If economic development flows to areas where prosperous home owners want to live, then dockland has a chance of success.

The LDDC has at least convinced people that dockland is not miles from all that is wonderful about London (though one journalist newly bussed-in to Rupert Murdoch's fortress in Wapping was said to have remarked that he was "going back to London" for a drink). The Docklands Light Railway has been an essential piece of infrastructure, locking the area into the public transport network. As we saw in Chapter 4, the Barking relief road and the Hackney Wick to M11 link road connect both ends of dockland to the national motorway network.

On the Isle of Dogs, it is already possible to believe that the dream will come true. Architects, freed from planning constraints, have run riot. Terry Farrell's wonderful post-modernist building for the Limehouse Studios must count as one of the finest things to be built in England since 1945. At times, it must be said, the hype can be overbearing. A leisure development on the North Quay of the West India Docks, for example, is scheduled to have not just a 400-room hotel but such wonders as a "festival market", a museum, an international food hall, restaurants, leisure theme pavilions, "a recreation of old Limehouse", and a dock for square-masted sailing ships.

There seem to me to be two unanswered questions about the development in dockland. The first is whether all the new activity will be no more than delicious raisins stuck in a distinctly unappetising dough. How will all this fun connect with the old East End to the north? Is it meant to do so at all? There are plenty who would argue that one of the main consequences of the tax breaks in dockland will be that investors will be even less likely to put their money in the old East End. Is that desirable? How will dockland avoid becoming a rich ghetto? It would be stupid to romanticise some of the least attractive parts of London, but it would be understandable if people stuck in council estates in Newham, Tower Hamlets and Southwark did not feel a little put out by the wealth and lifestyle of their new neighbours.

The second unanswered question is whether the success of the schemes in Wapping and the Isle of Dogs can be reproduced further east. Wapping is close to the City, and almost underneath the great tourist attraction of the Tower of London. St Katharine's Dock, just east of Tower Bridge, has been an example since 1973, when Taylor Woodrow built the Tower Hotel, of the way that private money can create a waterside leisure extravaganza. So LDDC plans in the Isle of Dogs have always had a ready-made model.

But as Reg Ward is always fair enough to say, it is not possible to hope that the same trick will work in the Royals. The scale of the problem there is much greater. The docks are too big to be turned into pleasure domes, surrounded by waterside homes from which young software designers walk to their offices. The Royals are much too far east to convince trendy young Londoners that they are really living in the heart of the city; Beckton and Silvertown might be in Essex for all the sense of central London that you find there.

There is already new housing around the Royals, and very nice it is. But it is laid out in a much more conventional style than further west, and presumably will appeal mainly to those who already live in Newham (an Asda superstore scheduled to open there soon will make this area more attractive for native east Londoners). As for the docks themselves, they have not yet seen the scale of interest shown in the Isle of Dogs, though that has not been helped by a squabble between the Port of London Authority and the LDDC as to who should develop which bit of the dockside land. Thus an awful lot hinges on the success of the Stolport, and that, as I argued in Chapter 4, is by no means assured. On the other hand, the Stolport may come good, and if it does industry and distribution centres might flock to the Royals. It will be close to the east London river crossing, and thus the channel ports, and have easy access to Stansted. I want to believe in dockland; but whereas I feel that the western part of it has by now cracked an indefinable credibility barrier, I cannot get out of my mind the thought that things may yet go badly wrong in the east.

The state of the City

For many people, including those who wish it well, the LDDC has made one decision which is at best a risky gamble, and at worst a monumental blunder. This is the green light that the LDDC board gave in autumn, 1985 to American developer G. Ware Travelstead. He plans to build a financial services centre on Canary Wharf, in the heart of the Isle of Dogs. The £1.5 billion scheme would eventually provide 10m square feet of floor space, much of it in three 400-foot tall towers. It has been surrounded with typical dockland hype. The LDDC's newspaper has claimed that it will generate 40,000 jobs, of which 31,000 will be "new" – the Henley Centre for Forecasting, called in to do a study of the site, put the figure even higher. And there are promised another 50,000 jobs in support services – enough, the LDDC has claimed, to "wipe out east London's high unemployment problem".

The doubters fall into three camps. First, there are those who just do not believe that the finance for such a scheme will be forthcoming. Some remember similar grandiose plans, ten years ago, for the Surrey Docks, which came to nothing. The second group consists of environmentalists, who claim that the huge circuses, towers and concrete wastes are quite out of character with London's essential nature. Canary Wharf, they say, will ruin the view from Greenwich across the Royal Naval College to the City. Terry Farrell's gem at Limehouse would have to be demolished. Might Mr Travelstead not have come up with a plan that was a little more sensitive to London's skyline?

The third group of sceptics make a quite different objection. They simply doubt whether the financial services industry can sustain the kind of growth that the backers of Canary Wharf predict. If it cannot, the scheme will either not be built or be built as an expensive white elephant. To see if this third group are right, we have to wander down the streets of the City, London's hidden world.

The City is chock-full of contrasts. It is both the most and the least meritocratic part of the London economy. A bright East End lad (not a lass; the City is still a man's world) with an eye to a punt and a head for numbers can make a fortune there, dealing on the Stock Exchange or broking at Lloyds's. Yet in some of the top merchant banks, like Hambro's or Baring's, you have to be a member of the founding family to get right to the top. It is both the oldest part of London – its street layout dates from early medieval times, with some streets following Roman roads – and the newest. It has seen more skyscrapers on the model of Chicago or New York than any other part of London, and it relies for its prosperity on computers and telecommunications. There is nothing incongruous in the City about those same people who owe allegiance to a livery company, whose charter may date back several centuries, making their living from the application of state-of-the-art electronic gadgetry.

Above all, the City is the place in London where God and Mammon co-exist. After the Great Fire of 1666 (commemorated by the Monument), Sir Christopher Wren built new St Paul's and 63 other churches. His pupil Nicholas Hawksmoor added another clutch. Yet within the shelter of these churches (many of Wren's, sadly, demolished by bombs and developers) is one of the world's greatest concentrations of unbridled money-making. It is quintessentially English (its government, the City Corporation, has no charter – it has just been there, running the City, for 600 years) and yet is one of the few parts of the British economy that is truly international in its outlook. Any day in the City you may see a gent in a silk top-hat stroll in front of banks from Japan, America or Europe.

To those who do not work there – work is the operative word, for on census night 1981 less than 6,000 people lived there, as compared with 128,000 in 1801 – the City can often appear a mystery. Hamish McRae and Frances Cairncross, in their excellent book *Capital City,* give a clue to its flavour. There are, they say, really two cities. First there are the big battalions; the clearing banks, the life assurance companies, and the Bank of England itself. These tend to be cautious and conservative. On the other hand, there are the City's cottage industries; the merchant banks, the stockbrokers, the money-market men, the Lloyd's underwriters and brokers. These, say McRae and Cairncross, have a quality which is anti-intellectual and clubby. They combine "considerable dealing skills with a casual, even cavalier attitude to risk and a pride in amateurishness. Everything is a gamble, for finance is such a boring pursuit that the only way to make it bearable is to treat it as a game". It is not an exaggeration to say that in large measure the future success of London's economy depends on City men winning the game they are now playing.

That game could be called International Money-go-round. There is nothing new about the City having to compete in the outside world. It achieved its pre-eminence as a financial centre in the early nineteenth century only by offering services that Amsterdam could not. It has always been involved in international trade. Its great growth in the eighteenth century was founded on the back of trading concerns like the East India Company, and as early as 1832 Nathan Rothschild could claim that "this country is in general bank to the whole world". But the explosion of world trade since 1945, coupled first with the growth of Japan as a major industrial and commercial centre, and then with the internationalisation that computers have brought to trade and finance, has placed the City under new pressures.

The degree to which international trade has come to dominate the City can be gleaned from some simple statistics. In 1975, the City's earnings from overseas amounted to just £1 billion; in 1985 more than £10 billion. In 1972 there were less than 200 foreign banks in the City; in 1984, 460. During the same time, the number of foreign security houses increased from 54 to 120. In total, British jobs in finance, banking and insurance have increased by nearly 500,000 in the last ten years. That growth has been shared between London and the rest of the south-east – indeed London's share of employment in finance actually fell from 45% in 1961 to 35% in 1981, as insurance companies decentralised their operations. But this was a falling share of a growing market. Employment in financial and professional services in London has grown by nearly 5% in the last decade; nearly 100,000 people are now employed in insurance, and probably close to 150,000 in banking.

Those figures, according to some commentators, might have been bigger had London taken an opportunity to capitalise on its international reputation by buying into American financial companies 15 years ago. The City now faces a last chance to reap the harvest that it has been tending for 300 years. As trade in securities – in bits of paper – becomes as international as trade in commodities, so most observers think that there will be room for only three major financial centres in the world. Two will be New York and Tokyo. Both have conventional stock markets that dwarf the City's; New York's is seven times as big by market capital value and Tokyo's three times. London may be the third, though it will face competition from Frankfurt and Paris.

To ensure that London wins the race to be Europe's representative in this global market, the government actively encouraged what is now commonly called the City Revolution. In 1983, shortly after the General Election victory, Cecil Parkinson, during his short tenure as Secretary of State for Trade and Industry, stopped a court case against the Stock Exchange's old-fashioned rule-book in return for an assurance that the Exchange would scrap fixed commissions on deals by the end of 1986. Late-1986 is now known in the City as the time of the Big Bang.

The thinking behind the City Revolution, in very simple terms, was as follows. Introducing negotiated commissions on each deal a stockbroker struck meant that he would have to compete with rival brokers for business on price as well as quality of advice. To thrive in a competitive world, each broker would have to find new markets, abroad and, just as crucially, at home. New markets at home might consist of persuading the British, who love investing in bricks and mortar (and have been encouraged by tax breaks to do so) to start putting their money in stocks, shares and bonds. Financial supermarkets, involving over-the-counter deals of shares in BP or Shell rather than in packets of Omo or All Bran, might thus spring up.

All this would be good for British business, because it would thus have available to it additional sources of finance; it might be good for the British economy, because creating a much wider class of share-owners would extend the commitment of all in the society to the success of industry and commerce; and it would be good for the City, because if they learnt how to sell securities to the British they might soon learn how to sell them, in the same way, to the French and Germans. As a side-effect (it would simply be naive to pretend that this was uppermost in anyone's mind) all this new economic activity would produce jobs; jobs in the Revolutionised trades themselves; jobs in fringe activities like the law; jobs in wine bars where all these handsome profits have to be drunk away – for that matter, I suppose, jobs in domestic services to take the burden of those both too tired from their exertions in the Square Mile to sweep the grate out, and rich enough to employ someone else to do it. To make this dream come true, all those who work in the City have had to get used to a changed way of life. By comparison with American or Japanese firms, London stockbrokers are not particularly large; to be able to afford to move into the new markets that beckon post-Big Bang, they have had to look for additional capital. That has led to a rash of mergers in the City as the big four clearing banks and the merchant banks have taken large shareholdings in stockbrokers. American banks have got involved too. Citicorp, for example, has bought a stake in Vickers da Costa, Chase Manhattan aims to buy two medium-sized brokers. European banks like Credit Suisse and Deutsche Bank have also picked up pieces of the action. Of the sizeable brokers, only Cazenove's, probably the most blue-blooded of all, has remained independent. In all cases, the mergers are designed both to inject capital into the brokers and to put together the infrastructure of the promised financial supermarkets, which will sell you everything from an overdraft to a home loan to a package of stocks and shares, and perhaps even a life insurance policy as well.

The extra capital is needed for both people and machines. Machines, because computers and telecommunications have made the world security market possible, and every firm who wants to play International Money-go-round needs the best equipment it can get. City firms were reckoned to have invested nearly £400m in new technology in 1984, and are assumed to want to spend 14% more in each of the three following years. Much of that new machinery cannot be fitted into the old buildings of the City (the real constraint is that the ceilings are too low to accommodate the miles of cable required), which is one reason for the attractions of dockland in general and Canary Wharf in particular.

People, because of the quite extraordinary transfer of personnel within the City during the last two years. "Researchers" – necessary qualifications, according to one jaundiced City friend of mine, bare literacy and passable numeracy – have been in particular demand. These are the bright young sparks who write stockbrokers' circulars on whether or not to buy, sell or hold a particular share. They are an indispensable tool for the journalist, too – most of the ones I ring up seem to be called Max, but I have never investigated this scientifically. As the market for shares is set to both expand and become more competitive, the skills of these young men are in ever increasing demand. People who were by no means badly paid are moving firms for new salaries of £200,000 and upwards – the kind of figures that hitherto would only be commanded in the madhouse money-market rooms of the banks, where you're burnt out at 30, or in the commodities exchanges. ("Gold is boring", said a commodity broker I know to a prospective employee. "Deal in anything else if you want to make the real money. And don't get married. It won't last.").

This has led to some amusing law cases, where a bank has bought a stockbroker on the strength of its existing research team only to find it poached by someone else a few weeks later. I once sat in a TV studio waiting-room with a very well known financial analyst who had just moved from Important Bank A to Important Bank B. The studio manager said: "We'll bill you on screen as X from Bank B". "Christ, no", said the whizzkid, "It's all in litigation; they'll sue me from here to kingdom come".

Does all this jockeying for marginal advantage make sense? It has been done to the background of much tut-tutting, and not just from puritans and left-wing politicians. A partner in one of the biggest merchant banks thinks that the transfer fees have done nothing for the City's reputation; they have made a business that should depend on trust and honour look cheap and tawdry. His opinion is that the Revolution is only really welcomed with enthusiasm by people under 40; older City hands have been heard to mutter that it might all end in tears.

And indeed it might. John Plender and Paul Wallace, in 'The Square Mile', another excellent book on the City, point out that there are – or should be – strict limits to the growth of popular capitalism in Britain. They quote estimates that 7m people have no savings; 17m have less than £260 (the minimum amount that you could punt on British Telecom, the first great popular share issue) and another 9m have too little to invest in a portfolio of shares sufficiently large (say, 20 companies) to spread the risk in a sensible way. Of the adult population, this leaves only 3m who might be really interested in owning shares – and of those, 1.8m already do. As against this pessimism, the government has decided to give people more control over the huge sums that many of them have locked up in pension schemes, which if put into shares might expand the market exponentially. Certainly within the last two years, buying shares has been the fashionable thing to do. Gone are the days when earnest young couples would move their families' meagre nest-egg out of casino capitalism and put it into good old dependable building societies. (Even if the fashion for shares had not changed, you couldn't do that now – the building societies are playing by the new rules as much as anyone else).

Arguably, a more substantial constraint on the growth of the City is the fact that its recent reputation has not been a happy one. In the early 1970s the boom in property prices spawned a host of get-rich-quick secondary banks, some of whose owners got very rich, very quick, and some of whose depositors, once the market collapsed in 1973-74, got very poor just as fast. Then, towards the end of the 1970s, there were rumours that all might not be well in the Lloyd's insurance market, where risks from all over the world (for ships, or for the modern-day equivalent of Bette Davis's eyes) are accepted. Those risks are shared among "names"; quite rich (but not necessarily excessively so) individuals who stake everything down to the legendary last pair of gold cufflinks on paying out should a policy fall due. For the last few years some names have been holding on to the cufflinks, and much else besides. They have been less than eager to pay up, having discovered that some of the Lloyd's brokers and underwriters who put business their way were playing less than honestly – and in some cases siphoning off enormous profits for themselves. On top of the problems of Lloyd's – not sorted out by the introduction of a chief executive from outside its magic circle – came the collapse of Johnson Matthey Bankers amid yet more allegations of fraud. This led to the call both from left-wing politicians, who have always hated the City as much as they have failed to understand it, and from those who want to see a thriving City, but with well-protected investors, for a tough regulatory body to check that the City was playing fair.

This is the latest manifestation of an old dilemma. In the past, the City's tradition of self-regulation, with each of its branches running its own affairs under the watchful but informal eye of the Bank of England, has probably served both investors and the City well. And if London really is to beat Frankfurt and Paris at International Money-go-round, it will need the kind of relatively relaxed regulatory structures that will enable players in the new game to take risks without constant bureaucratic interference. On the other hand, this relaxed air will only work so long as those in the City behave like gentlemen, and so long as the Bank of England can both make its worries heard, and know they will be acted upon.

The problem is that at the moment neither condition is seen to be met. The secondary banking scam, Lloyd's, and now the transfer fees, all tend to show that the City is not made up exclusively of word-is-my-bond gents; truth to tell, it never has been, for which we might all be profoundly grateful. And the Johnson Matthey scandal suggests that the Bank of England does not have the resources to play policeman to all sectors of the new City. These considerations would no doubt have made hands-on regulation more likely, quite apart from the Big Bang. That has made matters worse. By putting into one conglomerate different financial operations with different goals, a clear potential for conflicts of interest has arisen. This has led to much talk of "Chinese Walls" between one part of a new bank-cum-broker and another. At the same time, the potential for conflicts has given added bite to those who call for statutory controls on the City's business. A substantial burden has now fallen on the new Securities & Investments Board, a statutory body which will act as an umbrella under which self-regulation will continue. This may well be the best compromise that can be offered for now. But if the first few years of the Revolution are littered with yet more City scandals, and

yet more little old ladies losing everything down to their
last pair of gold-plated corsets, then the pressure for an
American-style Securities & Exchange Commission will
become irresistible.

Welcome, or something
Some of those Wren and Hawksmoor churches in the City
attract more than 10,000 tourists a year. But if visitors to
London really want to go east, they tend to stick to the
Tower of London and St Paul's Cathedral. In a good year
for tourists, the Tower attracts 300,000 visitors, and St
Paul's over 2.5m. In 1983, the British Museum got nearly
3m; the National Gallery about the same; and Westminster Abbey a little more than St Paul's. The Science
Museum and the Natural History Museum, Kensington's
twin helpmeets to all parents on a wet half-term holiday,
attracted 3.3m and 2.5m respectively. Down the road, the
Victoria & Albert pulled nearly 2m (but how many of
them, I wonder, bothered to walk just a little further and
have a look at the Brompton Oratory?).

London is one of the world's great tourist destinations.
In 1984, 8.4m people from abroad visited it, together with
about 14m visitors from elsewhere in Britain. First
analysis of the figures for 1985 suggest that that year will
see a 7% rise in the number of foreigners coming to the
capital. In 1984, those foreigners spent about £2.5 billion
in London, about 57% of the cash spent by foreign tourists
in the whole country. The Brits spent much less; only
about £600m. On the back of the strong dollar, tourists
from the USA rose by nearly 1m between 1982 and 1984;
it is too early to say what effect the see-saw in dollar rates
in 1986, and scare stories about terrorism in Europe (of
which London has mainly been free) has had on
American visitors. Cabbies, who know about these things,
thought there were less Americans in town at the
beginning of 1986 than there had been for a few years.

According to the London Visitor and Convention

Bureau, about 230,000 jobs are directly involved in tourism in the capital, and another 150,000 indirectly; of this total of 380,000 about 25% are part-time. The official figures can never be reliable, because counting a job as one in the "tourist" trade means making all kinds of assumptions about the relative consumption of each worker's output by native Londoners and tourists respectively. Anyway, the official figures take no account of the black economy, which could be worth another 50,000, mainly part-time, jobs.

However you count the figures, tourism is London's biggest industry outside public administration. It employs probably 10% of the city's workforce, and could employ more. The British Tourist Authority says that an expansionist policy for tourism might generate another 50,000 jobs in London. Yet this growing industry has, until quite recently, been unloved. Why?

There are two main reasons. The first is that mass tourism is thought to have spoiled some parts of town. The area around the Palace of Westminster can look a dreadful mess at the height of summer, with huge queues to get into the Houses of Parliament and crowds at Westminster Abbey. The corner of Bridge Street and Parliament Street is occupied by a downmarket cluster of souvenir shops which give the whole area a cheapskate feel. The same kind of shops pollute much of Piccadilly Circus and Leicester Square, where their effect is exaggerated by contrast with the flashy Trocadero arcade, with its Guinness World Records exhibition. Victoria, with both a bus station and a train station which serves the channel ports, is similarly flyblown. Madame Tussauds and the Tower are both prime locations for shady ice-cream and rubbish sellers, some of them, let us put it delicately, not unknown to the police. Bloomsbury and Bayswater have had their characters changed by tourism. Their terraces and squares are now increasingly given over to hotels, and their older residents can be made to feel unwanted.

The second reason for a suspicion of tourism as a motor for the London economy is the extent to which the industry has traditionally offered low pay and poor working conditions. The fragmentation of the industry, with many employees working in small hotels and restaurants, has discouraged trade-union organisation. Where unions have got off the ground, employers in the industry have often tried to bust them. At times – especially in the 1970s – the business relied on foreigners for much of its labour. This provided employers with an excuse to depress both wages and job security. Filipino chamber-maids are not notorious for complaining about the terms and conditions of their employment.

These two objections can be so powerful that even some of London's Conservative politicians, whom one would expect would be anxious to encourage any economic activity in the city, balk at the prospect of boosting tourism. Perhaps for that reason, London has only partially taken all the opportunities that this industry presents for growth. According to the London Visitor and Convention Bureau, for example, overseas visitors spent less in London (at constant 1975 prices) in 1984 than they did in 1977, 1978 or 1979.

This lack of steady growth is usually put down to factors outside the industry's control; in particular the volatility of the $/£ exchange rate. But that is only half the story. Every bit as important has been the lack of a strategy designed to make London a tourist base, whatever the exchange rate. Such a strategy would have a number of components. First, it would involve a commitment to a high-quality tourist industry – meaning one which, among other things, cracked down on the gimcrack and fly-by-night operators. There are, for example, far too many money-changers in the centre of town who are prepared to fleece foreign visitors with impunity. Next, it would require the protection of the most environmentally important sectors of Park and City. There is absolutely no point in building new high-rise hotels in central London, because many visitors come to the city to get away from the excesses of modernism. Indeed, there is little point in building new hotels, of any description, in the city centre. Of the 135,000 or so beds in "serviced accommodation" in London, no less than 60% are in the three boroughs of Westminster, Kensington and Camden (in the case of the latter, mainly in Bloomsbury). Another 6% are in Hillingdon, serving Heathrow. The time is well past for a decentralisation policy for hotels; dockland provides one obvious location, but so do Richmond, Hammersmith and Hampstead – all are areas with excellent public transport links to Park and City. In an ideal world, hotels in these outlying districts would cater mainly for lower-income tourists. London's room prices are high by international standards, and not enough thought has been given to providing good quality accommodation for those like students, who will come back to the city time and time again if only they are treated properly. One part of treating them properly would be to give them what they want when they want it. London suffers from Britain's outmoded laws on licensing, and its tourist trade would benefit if there was further liberalisation of both Sunday trading and the opening hours of pubs and restaurants.

The strategy outlined here now has more of a chance of being put into practice than it has had for many years. Nationally, the government is committed to the tourist industry in particular and to deregulation of shop and – maybe – pub hours as well. It has built a new convention centre in a handsome building behind Parliament Square (though the two major convention centres, at Earl's Court and Olympia, will continue to have their growth limited by west London's chronic traffic problems). The GLC, which could never bring itself wholeheartedly to encourage the tourist industry, has gone.

Most important of all, the conservationists in London know that the success of the tourist industry depends on their success in preserving its old character. There are some signs that that perception has slowly dripped into the minds of policy-makers, who seem less keen on the wholescale redevelopment of inner-city areas than they were. When all these factors come together, facilities designed with one eye on potential tourists can be a godsend to native Londoners as well. Covent Garden is the proof.

Once the old fruit and vegetable market moved to Battersea, the authorities had to decide what to do with the space around Inigo Jones's piazza just north of the Strand. Mercifully, local pressure stopped comprehensive redevelopment, which would have turned this crucial area into a featureless landscape of office blocks. The fruit and vegetable halls were preserved and converted into shops and restaurants. That acted as a catalyst for the whole area, in two ways. First, it made it much easier to fight for continued use of old buildings like the Jubilee Hall (just to the south of the Piazza) and a delightful triangle of Victorian buildings at Seven Dials. Second, the success of the Piazza encouraged shops and restaurants into the nearby streets. Covent Garden is now the liveliest part of Park and City. Uniquely for the centre of town, it provides a space where it is possible to enjoy oneself (weather permitting) outside as well as indoors. It is, of course, attractive to tourists. But as any Saturday afternoon, any time of the year, demonstrates, it is loved by Londoners too. More developments like that – and the next great challenge will be the Smithfield site north of the City – will confirm that the most promising of London's industries can serve its own population as well as it serves those who want to visit the city.

Street-Cred

I first met Mark and Syrie in the tea-shop just off Carnaby Street. This needs some explaining. Carnaby Street had ten minutes of fame in the 1960s – Swinging London days – when it was the centre for the weird fashions of the time. Remember the craze for military uniforms, and the shop called "I was Lord Kitchener's Valet"? It then turned into a tawdry parody of its golden days, and, despite a recent effort to spruce it up, remains a collection of rip-off shops selling knick-knacks and Brummagem. It is not where you would expect to find a genuine old English tea shoppe, complete with chintz chairs and horse brasses. Yet one is there.

That was where Mark met Syrie when they were both unemployed and in their early twenties. They decided to go into the fashion business, and started cutting up everything from old tapestries to tea towels in the bathroom upstairs. Within a year they had spreads in *Vogue* and *The Face,* had two pages on their style in *Country Life* (the magazine of England's rural gentry, most of whom would run a mile if they had ever seen the terrible duo) and had sold their stuff in every top shop from Harrods to Bloomingdales. They received standing ovations from the world's fashion press and some of its great designers when they presented their first major collections in 1985.

The secret of their success has been to take elements of London's street life – the punks, the souvenirs, the sense of wild and eclectic style – and turn it into high-quality clothes. They are as good an example as I can give of the most exciting part of London's economy – street-cred.

Street-cred (an already old-hat term – Mark tells me that "Skat" will be the new style-word) is short for street-credibility. That is what you need if you are to survive anywhere where young Londoners are gathered together. It has now supplanted "trendy" – a word nobody who is trendy would ever dream of using – as the description of a certain lifestyle that is indefinably and uniquely London's

Trendy was a word for the 1960s and early 1970s. *Time Out* magazine once defined it as "democratic affluence", and the emphasis should be placed on democratic. The original trendies considered themselves to have a political outlook which eschewed both elitism and business – in the '60s and '70s, after all, most young Brits thought those vices were synonymous.

Street-cred is quite different. My own definition of it is that it means that its possessor is sharp, on-the-make, ready to do a deal, and businesslike. It is quite possible to be street-cred and socialist, at least socialist of the Livingstone/GLC kind (Roy Hattersley does not have street-cred) but it is not necessary. Bob Geldof's Band Aid had street-cred – its hallmark was Geldof's passion for squeezing deals out of fat-cat businessmen. Red Wedge, the Billy Bragg-led tour of rock muscians for the Labour Party, does not. It is possible to be street-cred and mystical. A group of some of London fashion's most influential people – I kid you not – periodically chant Buddhist mantras together. Indeed, the London Buddhist Centre in Bethnal Green is run by a bunch of delightful street-cred men who own a shop, a couple of restaurants, and have a business worth over £500,000 a year. Above all else, street-cred is meritocratic rather than democratic. Those who have it believe they should flaunt it, and if they can flaunt it, they might as well make money out of it.

I hand the palm to Tony Elliott, publisher of *Time Out*, for first realising how street-cred (though he did not coin the word) might change the face of London. His magazine had catered to trendy young London since the late 1960s. Like everyone in that environment, he was horrified when Mrs Thatcher won the 1979 election. But within a year he had realised that her victory had symbolised something quite important. Young London was no longer very interested in whatever was the fashionable political or pressure group nostrum of the week. Young Londoners wanted to consume. The fact that so many have conspicuously consumed their way through recession has been the main thing that has made their last seven years bearable.

Tony Elliott's insight was put to the test, though not in

a way he would have chosen. In 1981 there was a strike at *Time Out* over the issue of equal pay for all – a classic '60s and '70s cry. Many of the journalists left to start a new weekly paper called *City Limits*. This is an excellent product, excellently written. But it still assumes that what makes young Londoners tick is a dedication to politics and radical pressure groups. It sells 25,000 copies a week. *Time Out,* which has gone like a train for the consumer end of the market, sells three times that number.

Once consumption became the thing that everyone liked doing, production was bound to follow. Businessmen spotted markets for new goods and products, and street-cred consumers themselves felt duty-bound to turn their ideas into cash. The upshot is that London has become a much more entrepreneurial city than it was a decade ago. But entrepreneurial in a specific way. London is now, above all, a creative centre. Take, as an important example, its advertising agencies, renowned the world over for their creative skills. Advertising now employs over 20,000 people in London (about 60% of the national total), and many of those agencies – Saatchi & Saatchi the best known, but not necessarily the best creatively – have made major acquisitions in foreign markets. Some of the best of Britain's crop of young film directors (like Ridley Scott and Alan Parker) owe their success to a training in the hard world of advertising.

It has been clear to those in the know for ages – though scandalously unrecognised by government – that the creative and cultural industries of London were providing the base for major growth. Nearly 50,000 books a year are now published in Britain – more than ever before – and of that total some 35% are exported. British records make up a quarter of the world's output, from an island that has only 6% of the world market. Over 30,000 people are employed in the London music business. But it was not until 1982 that the potential of this creativity became obvious.

That was the year that Channel 4 was launched as a TV station unique in the world. In 1980 and 1981 I spent some time working for Phillip Whitehead, then a Labour MP, and virtually the only parliamentarian who believed that a channel could be set up which relied for much of its input from small, independent programme-makers. He told everyone who cared to listen that London was bursting with talent to make films, features, documentaries, comedy, and anything else that you might reasonably wish to watch in your living room (and a fair amount that you might not). The great and the good poured cold water on his enthusiasm. Yet Channel 4 has succeeded in carving out a distinct role for itself beyond anything that even the optimists believed possible. And, like Covent Garden, it has acted as a catalyst of tremendous significance. Comedians, musicians, political commentators – anyone with a bright idea – now knows that if they get that idea on video, and keep their standards high, they have the chance of a platform. London's street-cred culture has responded magnificently.

The street-cred economy has harnessed, to an extent never done before, the innate sense of style that young Britons have shown since the early 1960s. And for this, thank, in large measure, the art colleges. If I had to choose one site to symbolise the new British economy it would be St Martin's School of Art, in the middle of the Soho/Covent Garden street-cred village. Out of St Martin's and its peers have come the fashion designers. Ten years ago the idea that London's fashions would be regarded as important as those from Paris or Italy would have seemed a bad joke. But they are now; designers like Bodymap, Jasper Conran, Wendy Dagworthy and Katharine Hamnett have marshalled London's street-life (remember Ms Hamnett's outsize T-shirts?) and turned it into a style that Paris, Milan or New York just can't match. Cheap chic is what London is about. It is typical of the delightful chaos of the street-cred economy that London's fashion collections are usually held not in some glittery hall but in a tent.

And then there is the music. Punk rock will one day be seen as among the most significant social phenomena in twentieth-century Britain. In its heyday, between 1975 and 1978, it was misinterpreted by just about every observer over 30. Punk had nothing to do with working-class kids on the council estates rebelling against arty rock. It was, like most twentieth-century social movements in Britain, art-school led. Malcolm McLaren, the Sex Pistols' Svengali, was an artist. Vivienne Westwood, his partner, was a fashion designer. The Pistols' first gig was at St Martin's; all the members of the original Clash were art students. What distinguished this movement from earlier art college ones was that, this time, the students were entrepreneurs as well. The music business was the perfect target, having grown staid and self-congratulatory on the back of the English super-groups of the 1960s.

Punk changed all that. Never mind that some of the music was rotten, or that some of its stars fell into exactly the same traps as rock stars before them. Punk created the illusion that anything was possible – you really could make a record, you really could design a sleeve – and once that happened people spent the next few years making the illusion a reality. Friends whose first commissioned work was designing sleeves for punk bands now design films for Hollywood – that's the street-cred economy for you.

Not everyone within this economy will grow, and some of its sharpest observers worry about whether it will ever be as serious and grown-up as the industries in Germany, Japan or the USA. I would warn against pessimism. Growth has come in the most unlikely places. You would not have bet, for example, that the one-night-a-week nightclub business that grew up in the late 1970s, when students took over clubs for the latest month-long craze (remember the New Romantics?) would breed successful businessmen. But it has. Steve Strange and Rusty Egan

went on from the Blitz to open the huge Camden Palace
night-spot in Mornington Crescent. Watch, now, Gaz
Mayall. This young man started out selling clothes in
Kensington Market, and now runs a great once-a-week
club where he plays all kinds of wonderful blues. He
already charters boats across the channel for all-night
sessions, and from his extraordinary Aladdin's cave of a
basement flat in Bayswater (where he strides around in a
cocked hat, showing visitors a record collection fit to
make your eyes pop) plots his next move into the big
time. He'll make it all right.

For established businessmen skilful enough to tap this
lode, there are rich pickings to be made. Ask Richard
Branson. The secret of the success of his Virgin Group,
whose turnover is now nearly £200m a year, has been to
stay close to his core market. That market is youngsters
who want to have fun – whether in his clubs, in his
record stores, or by flying his 'planes to the USA. He has
shown just how much can be made from tapping young
London; so have the ad agencies; so have the TV and film
companies; so, even, have the travel companies (Harry
Goodman's Intasun travel company, with its sun-and-sex
offshoot Club 18-30, could only be dreamed up by a
Londoner for Londoners).

Street-cred spells a quirky, oddball creativity; one that
makes few concessions to older established ways of doing
business. I like to think that it is the business of
tomorrow. Small-scale, dependent on brain power, yet
happy to use the latest technology (just watch those kids
play with their ghetto blasters and synthesisers), friendly,
anarchic. Put it together with the black economy, the
M25, dockland, the City, and tourism, and any gloom
about London's future disappears like the autumn leaves
in St James's Park. If only conventional financiers and
politicians could see it, they would find that London had
just what it takes to be the creative business centre of the
next century.

7
PLAY

On a bitterly cold Saturday in February, at 11.00 pm, I went recently to Leicester Square underground station. The cinemas and theatres had just finished their last shows; ticket queues were 30 yards long; the escalators were double-banked with crowds and the platforms lined five persons deep. One train followed another into the station and took off the first few layers of people; new crowds quickly took their place. Two weeks later, I spent a warm Saturday afternoon on the Covent Garden Piazza. Even the lousiest of buskers drew crowds; some shops were so full they had to ration visitors; everywhere people stood outside the pubs drinking pints of lager, or wandered round the stalls munching fast food.

Odd, this. According to many, London is the capital city of a nation close to economic ruin. Yet its centre just doesn't feel that way. On the contrary, in ten years it has gone through nothing less than a leisure revolution, and is now the pleasure dome of Europe. Either the economic position is not as bad as some of the figures show, or Londoners have made a quite conscious decision to conspicuously consume today, lest tomorrow they be unemployed. Whatever the explanation, one thing stands out. Poor quality leisure and recreation is no longer good enough for the Londoner. He or she wants excellence. Those who have provided it have been amply rewarded.

Food, food; drink, drink
When Raymond Postgate, a historian and socialist of note, first launched *The Good Food Guide* in the years of

142

post-war austerity, he did so in the belief that good food
and drink should be the prerogative of everyman – and
that everyman was being bilked. Even in London, which
in this respect was light years ahead of the rest of Britain,
good eating was limited to the big West End hotels, a
handful of old and expensive restaurants and a host of
gimcrack Italian and French bistros, heavy with checked
tablecloths and gay posters, and serving food whose
dominant feature was the colour brown. As late as 1981,
the inspectors of the *Guide* could only find some 150
restaurants in town that they were prepared to
recommend. They now list nearly 300. Hardly a week
goes by without another smart place opening its doors to
a new crowd. And not just in the West End; you may now
choose between a variety of excellent restaurants all over
west London (the Fulham and Brompton Roads have a
score of top-class eateries), in Richmond, in Hampstead,
even, for heaven's sake, south of the river.

The old hotels are still there, of course. The Ritz gives
you a view of Green Park; the Savoy of the river. The
Dorchester delights with a *menu surprise,* created by
master chef Anton Mosimann and presented with great
good humour by its staff. And best of all is the Connaught,
which serves superlative food in an atmosphere that is
gracious without being fawning. But the great restaurants
of the 1940s and 1950s have now been left behind by a
new generation of chefs and their businessmen backers.
The worst meal I have had in London in the last year (and
one of the most expensive) was in a restaurant that my
mother-in-law would have killed to get taken to in the
1930s.

Of the new generation of top-of-the-range restaurants,
none epitomises the new London's obsession with
high-quality leisure, even at a price, so much as Le
Gavroche, in Mayfair. Its chef, Albert Roux, has won
Britain's first three-star award from Michelin. The
basement restaurant is sumptuous. Pastels abound; the
tables are not on top of each other – and the food is

spectacular.

But the point of the success of Roux and his brother Michel (who serves equally delicious food at the Waterside Inn at Bray) lies not just in the cooking. The Roux brothers and their backers have been able to bankroll a set of very expensive restaurants in town (with chefs whom they often trained themselves) in the sure knowledge that a market will beat a path to their door. They have, in other words, been prepared to back a hunch that Londoners have changed the way in which they spend their money, and they have been proved handsomely right.

Yes, but; are not these highly priced eating-houses an irrelevance to most Londoners? When you have to shell out £100 for a meal for two (as, with wine, you could easily do for dinner at Le Gavroche) the market must be so narrow as to be limited to tourists or those who can flash expense accounts. Yet I am always struck in even the most expensive restaurants by how many quite ordinary people seem to be prepared to use them for a fun celebration. Anyway, the objection misses the point. The flair and excellence of London's top restaurants has fired a generation of both chefs and businessmen to provide much cheaper eating-places, of a range and variety that would have astounded Postgate.

Take Bob Payton, a Chicago adman who got tired of being unable to find his native town's deep-pan pizza in London. So he started to make his own, in a small cafe in Crown Passage. Once he outgrew that he moved to bigger premises in Hanover Square, opened a rib place in Knightsbridge, an upmarket (and unsuccessful, in my view) fish and chip joint in the Charing Cross Road, and turned a handful of pubs into lively, politely run food-and-drink bars of the kind that are two-a-penny in the USA but have been scarce in London. Payton's restaurants are (though he would deny it) good value for unexceptional food. But the food craze has spawned plenty of places only a little more costly than Payton's which are very good indeed.

It has been particularly heartening to see – in Covent Garden, Soho and Kensington – the growth of all-day brasseries, prepared to sell you anything from a croissant and coffee to a full meal, at any time. A modest change in the licensing laws would spawn many more. Further up the market is the class of restaurant that is transforming London; these are places that appeal to the young professional who travels abroad and who is prepared to have a night out (in a way which few Britons over 40 are) in a restaurant – and which give you good food without costing an arm and a leg. They range from small places that can only do meals for about 20 or 30 (a feature of the Brompton Road scene) to places like Langan's Brasserie, which serves something like 400 meals a day, at great value, with maximum efficiency, and with the added bonus of the possibility of seeing either the proprietor drunk or Michael Caine (his partner) sober.

All this, and the ethnic restaurants too. When food in Britain was on its uppers, the only places you could find good cheap food was in Indian and Chinese restaurants. When I lived in Chicago in the early 1970s, the small expatriate community used to gather in the only Indian restaurant in town to try and remember what home was like. The ethnic (should one say colonial?) restaurants, too, have capitalised on the Londoner's new discernment by going upmarket. In 1981, only 18% of *Good Food Guide* restaurants in London served non-European food; now 34% do, and that, remember, is in a sample whose total size has nearly doubled. Upmarket in quality, but with only a few exceptions (of which more below) not costing the earth. Places like the India Club on the Strand, where pictures of Gandhi and Nehru peer down on plain formica tables, will feed you some of the best vegetarian food, mopped up with the most delicious puris, all for less than a fiver. Or try Khan's, on Westbourne Grove, a packed madhouse of a place that I always think is the closest London gets to an eighteenth-century chop-house.

For China-hands, dim sum is a must; £4 will get you a lunchtime feast at the New World or Chuen Cheng Ku, great barns of places packed with Chinese families and local office-workers guzzling dumplings and webbing from the never-ending supply of trolleys.

To a limited extent, this good value has been threatened by the growth of "boutique" Chinese and Indian restaurants – the Indian ones mainly in Covent Garden and Soho (though with one of the best at the Indian-owned Bailey's Hotel in Gloucester Road), the Chinese ones in Kensington. The Indians are better value; the Last Days of the Raj, run by a co-operative (who, legend has it, wanted to call their brainchild "The Empire Strikes Back") was the first from the sub-continent, and is still one of the best. Too many of the Chinese boutique eating-places serve the same food you would get in Lisle Street – not Gerrard Street, which though the heart of modern Chinatown is not crammed with good restaurants – at three times the price. They even try to serve you wine, when they should be concentrating on decent tea (a grave failing of Chinese restaurants in Britain, the tea; much too insipid).

If, however, wine is your tipple, then London is your place – as it has been for three centuries. Truth to tell, London is much too good a place for any kind of booze. Iago knew a thing or two when he said that nobody could outdrink the Anglo; compare us to the foreigners on any cross-channel ferry for the modern truth of his words.

Not all toping need be so ungracious. Drop in to Berry Bros & Rudd on St James's Street, which is probably the finest eighteenth-century interior in London, and ask them to bring a bottle of claret up from the cellar. Intelligent, unchauvinist Frenchmen (I know one; maybe two) will concede that London is, for readily available range and quality, now the wine-consuming capital of the world – and this is in a country whose consumption is still small (though growing fast) compared with other European countries. It is the range and quality of wine in

London that is breathtaking. Within a walk of my office are three wine stores with a stupendous range; within five minutes' drive of my home another three. I would maintain that London's restaurants today offer a finer choice of wine than those in any other comparable city. London party-goers consume the stuff with abandon; one of my little pleasures in life is to watch the Sunday morning ritual of wine-bottles-into-dustbins as I stroll back from the newsagent.

Both wine bars and wine warehouses have sprung up to meet the new demand. The former are often to be found along the river, in places such as Wapping and Battersea. The latter, increasingly, are all over town. The conventional theory for the success of the wine bar is that they are much less threatening places for women than pubs. Men don't get so aggressive in wine bars; though that, I suppose, is because aggressive men don't drink wine. I suspect this explanation is too coy. The real reason, surely, is that wine bars are now the best pulling places in London. In the first few years of the new Covent Garden, watching the assignations on a Friday night at the downstairs bar of the Café des Amis du Vin was one of the best sports in town. But the bars' potential for setting up sex later in the evening is often greater than their value for money. Britain's law-makers have been slow to recognise that their children are throwing down bottles of wine like there was no tomorrow, and so have failed to stipulate that a wine glass must contain a certain amount of liquid. Thus even as you are eyeing up your latest conquest, you are likely to be ripped off, which I suppose serves many wolves right.

Would the burst of interest in food and drink have happened without the redevelopment of Covent Garden? I doubt it; or at least I doubt if it would have happened to the same extent. Just five years after the refurbished Piazza opened, it has already become fashionable to knock it. But by dumping into the middle of the West End a temple to the fripperies of life it became possible to test whether ordinary Londoners would spend their cash on those things in which a sniffy establishment thought they would never show an interest. The tastes of ordinary Brits were revealed to be a good deal higher than their masters had expected. The success of Covent Garden has now spilt over the Charing Cross Road into Soho. Play has always been one of Soho's main businesses. The sex shops and parlours are still there, adapting their offerings continually to the latest fashion. In an effort to attract the mass market of the 50p punter in place of the shrinking £50 one, peep-shows replaced many strip-clubs a few years ago. They are now fading from the scene to be replaced by nude bed-shows – still for less than £1. And the district continues to boast some genuine old-fashioned brothels.

But the new Soho is less dependent on sex; and the sex is less offensive than it was. Determined, if belated, action by Westminster council, who has enforced new licensing laws and regulations on window displays, has cut down the number of shops and parlours and made their public face less sleazy. In have come new wine bars and restaurants. One indicator of Soho's new fashionable status is the number of private clubs for media people there. London has always had clubs for the rich and establishment-minded; crusty places in St James's or Pall Mall where (with the exception of the Reform Club) women are still a rarity. But apart from the Garrick, catering for well-heeled theatre people and journalists, there has been little offered to London's new profession-als. That changed in the 1970s when the Zanzibar was opened on Long Acre in Covent Garden, appealing directly to admen, publishers, the younger breed of journalist and all the other denizens of the street-cred economy. Significantly, the clubs that have taken the Zanzibar's formula further have set up in Soho – Old Compton Street and its surrounds is now where you can see to best effect London's young whizzkids shop (in Camisa's for pasta, Delmonico's for wine, Moroni's for foreign papers and the Algerian coffee shop for coffee from Algeria and elsewhere), have lunch, and get plastered on Côtes de Provence.

Soho used to be famous, too, for the quality of its pubs. There are still some good Victorian ones there, though rather too many are dominated by people who want you to think they are a character, and by impressionable young men who want to bore you at their next party with long tales of how they know this Soho pub that is just full of characters.

In this respect, I think Soho is symptomatic of the whole of London. It is time to blow the whistle on the pub. Most in London are smelly and smoky, serving bad food in Victorian and Edwardian palaces that they do not deserve. Some, of course, have moved with the times. Especially in New Bow Bells, you can find massive places with plenty of entertainment. In some suburbs, especially in Waterside, there are plenty of pubs that are genuinely friendly in the way that pubs outside London are. But most of the neighbourhood pubs in Brookstown, Micawber and Northern Heights are pretty uninteresting, except for those which have acquired a reputation for somewhere where you simply must go if you are in Hampstead, or Highgate, or Dulwich, or wherever. These then tend to be crowded and expensive. Then there are the Kensington pubs dominated by inverted snobbery – full from six o'clock with Sloane Rangers and their escorts drinking beer just like they did in the butteries of their Oxford colleges.

Only a very few pubs in central London give you both good beer, the choice of well-kept wine if you want it, and the possibility of something other than mousetrap cheese and stale bread to eat. As everyone knows which they are, they tend to be unbearably crowded. If you think this heterodoxy is ill-founded, ask yourself a simple question. When was the last time you visited one of these shrines to friendliness and fellowship and had a decent conversation with someone you'd never met before? When, for that matter, did you ever pick anyone up in a pub? The breweries may say that they have done all they can to cater for a changing market, but the growth of the wine bars, and the number of Londoners who prefer to do their drinking at home, both point, decisively, the other way.

High, middle, low

"London", said Sir William Rees-Mogg, Chairman of the Arts Council, in 1984, "is probably the greatest artistic metropolis of the modern world, challenged only by New York, and bearing more than comparison with any continental European city". Quite a claim. True?

Yes, probably. London has four full-scale symphony orchestras and innumerable chamber groups and choirs, which together provide concerts unrivalled for variety anywhere in the world. It has two theatre companies, the National Theatre and the Royal Shakespeare, which in their mammoth buildings may on any one day have six shows in repertory and be playing two or three others on transfer in the West End. Both companies would generally be admitted to be among the world's finest collection of actors, directors and designers. Another 40 largish theatres in the commercial sector are likely to be in use at any one time. On a week chosen at random in March, 1986, they were supplemented by 96 fringe and studio shows.

London has two opera houses, one of which – the Royal Opera House, Covent Garden – attracts the top names of the world, while the other – the English National Opera – has an enviable record of finding exciting and accessible productions of both classics and undiscovered works. It has 170 art galleries, at least three of which – the National Portrait Gallery, the Tate and the National Gallery – are top-class. The city attracts the same international exhibitions that tread the circuit from Paris to New York. It has two world famous modern dance companies (though its classical ballet could not be called Britain's gift to the world). In any week, over 250 films are likely to be playing in its cinemas.

Yet there is an air of unease about this wealth of artistry; an unease shared by both those who work in the arts and by those who enjoy them. At its simplest, the arts in London demonstrate a paradox that runs through much of the city's life, and one that takes us right back to Paul Theroux's suggestion that London is not really a city at all. The basic question is: is London British, or is it international? Until an answer is given, the extent of public and government support for the arts will continue to be bedevilled with doubt.

For if London's arts are to be seen through the spectacles of the rest of Britain, then there are good grounds for saying that they hog too much of the cake. The Arts Council has always had a brief to provide support for the arts all over Britain as well as to build an artistic showcase in the capital. It was the feeling that the second of these objectives had been achieved to the detriment of the first that lay behind the Council's commitment to a dispersal and decentralisation of its funding in 1984.

The facts speak for themselves. According to The Artists' Directory, in 1985 those 170 art galleries accounted for 30% of all the galleries in the country – and in terms of hanging space that must be a gross understatement. In 1980-81, when the Policy Studies Institute looked at subsidy of the arts, it found (in a conclusion with which the Arts Council does not quibble) that the Council's expenditure per head of population in London was 3½ times more than the region next best-supported, and nine times more than the region least well-endowed. In the Arts Council's report for 1984-85, some £98m pounds of expenditure on the arts was accounted for. Of that total, over £18m was spent on London's two opera houses; £7m went to the National Theatre, and over £5m was split between the Royal Shakespeare Company's operations in London and

Stratford-on-Avon. The London Orchestra Concert Board, which allocates money to the four symphony orchestras, got £1.3m. Another £1.6m went to the Greater London Arts Association to fund its own schemes – and countless sums went to London-based companies and galleries. On broad brush reckoning, the Arts Council thinks that about half its annual expenditure goes to London.

There is little wonder that the rest of the country complains. But say, by contrast, that the real comparison is with great foreign centres. Does London stand up? What do its people get for the cash that the Arts Council spends? First, naturally, they get a whopping subsidy on their ticket prices (ranging in 1982-83, from £2.40 a seat at the concert halls to about £3 at the National and RSC theatres and – wait for it – some £18 on each opera ticket sold). But, in addition to this, I think that they often get superb art. Take the Royal Shakespeare Company as an example. It goes without saying that its Shakespearean productions are second to none in the world, and so they should be. But nobody who sat through *Nicholas Nickleby* or who in the last year has seen the chilling performance of Laclos' *Liaisons Dangereuses* could doubt that the company has the knack of turning up star performers in star productions. The ranks of those now just making it big in the British theatre – like Roger Rees, Juliet Stevenson or Bob Peck – would be very much thinned had it not been for the RSC's ability to bring on new talent. Established actors like Alan Howard, Ian McKellen and Judi Dench have done their best work for Trevor Nunn and Terry Hands, the company's joint directors.

The National Theatre had a similar record from 1963 to 1976, in its temporary home at the Old Vic. But it got off to a somewhat rocky start in its new theatre on the South Bank. Yet there, too, the London theatre-goer has been well served. Though the National may have had less smashes than the RSC, some of its shows – like *The Oresteia* and the revival of *Guys and Dolls* – have been fantastic, and it has had a run of successes in the Cottesloe, the smallest of the three auditoria on the site.

The subsidy buys the London concert-goer enormous choice. In my random week in March, 1986 there were nearly 100 classical concerts in town. That number may decline. The Arts Council said in 1984 that it was unwilling to support all four symphony orchestras – the London Symphony, the Royal Philharmonic, the Philharmonia and the London Philharmonic – especially as the city also has the BBC Symphony (which comes into its own during the promenade season) and orchestras at Covent Garden and the English National Opera. The Council wanted one of the four symphony orchestras to go to the east Midlands; no chance. Yet it is not just the provinces that suffer from the amount of music in London. Arguably, Londoners do too, for despite having perhaps the most discerning audience in modern Europe, the capital has never been able to boast an orchestra of the quality of Chicago's or Berlin's. That must be because the available pool of talent has been diluted.

If the concert-goer is spoilt for choice by Arts Council largesse, then the opera-lover is just plain spoilt. Without anyone that I know getting to grips with the phenomenon, London is starting to go opera-mad. The most surprising people now pontificate about arias at the drop of a hat. *Tribune,* the left-wing weekly, now reviews opera; Channel 4 covers it well, and you can't get more street-cred than that. Picking up on this new kind of interest, the English National Opera has developed what looks like a policy of the demystification of opera. All its performances are in English, and many of them presented in a fresh and modern way; the Jonathan Miller *Rigoletto* set in 1950s Little Italy was unforgettable. The ENO has now tied all this together with some of the best advertisements around, showing teenagers arriving at the Coliseum in jeans on a motorbike. The image that the ENO consciously seeks could hardly be further from a gala night at Covent Garden, with London's rich and philistine hanging over the edge of their boxes dripping jewels.

Are the huge sums of public money given to the national companies spent wisely? Well, at Mrs Thatcher's behest, both the RSC and Covent Garden had their operations scrutinised in detail by a senior civil servant and came out with flying colours. Where the taxpayer might feel a little more sceptical is in relation to the capital cost of the national companies. The National Theatre must have seemed a splendid building when it was designed by Sir Denys Lasdun in the 1960s. Now it just looks like a monument to everything that was awful about modernist architecture, its great hulking concrete walls weeping in the rain. And there must be some doubt as to whether the Barbican Centre, built at a cost of more than £150m, was really necessary. The London Symphony Orchestra has its home there, as does the RSC. The halls are indeed spectacular – I know of no auditorium with such good sight lines as the Barbican's main theatre – but the case for moving those companies from their cramped quarters in the West End must be said, so far, to be not proven. Certainly the Barbican Centre has not yet revitalised the area surrounding it.

There are those who say that the arts in London will always be in a state of panic so long as the great national companies rely so much on taxpayers' money which can be withdrawn whenever the Chancellor of the Exchequer feels so inclined. Of course, they all try for commercial sponsorship too, but there is now a school that says that if only they marketed themselves better they could get lots of individual and corporate subscriptions like the Royal Academy has done. Short of a major change in the tax laws, there seems little prospect of this move to American-style funding; that means, among other things, that the inherent tension between London and the provinces will continue.

For the commercial theatre in the West End these arguments are somewhat academic. It has never been able to rely on subventions from the public purse, and has failed to persuade the government to remove value-added tax from theatre tickets. Quite recently, the West End scene was decidedly gloomy. Too many theatres were dark, tickets were not being marketed aggressively, and levels of investment in both theatres and productions were low. Theatres were beginning to show their age; most of the West End houses are now a hundred years old, and without a ready supply of cash the old gilted and galleried structures can rapidly go downhill. (Yet they are so worth preserving; give me the most moth-eaten, underground theatre in the West End for a hundred of the newer ones, like the Mermaid or the Shaw).

Helped, without question, by the tourist boom of the mid-1980s, the worst is now behind the West End. Whereas in 1982 an average of only 33 stages had shows playing at any one time, in 1985 the figure was 45. Annual attendances have edged over the 10m mark. This has been achieved in the main by clever marketing; by tie-ups with British Rail, by concessionary tickets for students and above all by a half-price same-day booth in Leicester Square, just in front of the embarrassing statue of Charlie Chaplin. And though the success has had its critics – some have complained that the main marketing gimmick has been to cram in American musicals – the main result of the new entrepreneurialism has been an upswing in investment both in theatres and in new shows. That has got to be good news for the future.

Though many smaller theatre groups receive small amounts of subsidy either from the Arts Council or from local councils (which, naturally, vary substantially in their generosity) the fringe and studio theatres have always had to be entrepreneurial, relying on finding new writers with shows that might transfer to the West End. The cinema, too, has had to live in an unprotected environment; compared to theatre, drama or dance, it receives pitifully small amounts of subsidy. London has lost hundreds of cinemas since the days when film was the main form of mass entertainment in the capital. The British still watch films; but they watch them at home, either scheduled on television, or by means of a VCR. Britain took to video more quickly than any other country, Japan not excluded. Part of the reason for that must have been the lack of investment in cinemas in the 1960s and 1970s, leaving too many suburban houses tatty, dirty and deserted.

Yet if those who own a cinema bother to treat their clientele well, then Londoners will respond, just as they have to those who have given good value for money in restaurants. Plenty of people still want to see a film on a big screen, and on a Friday or Saturday night in west London (which is without question the part of London best served for cinema; between Notting Hill Gate and the King's Road are more than ten screens, with no chain owning more than one cinema) it is not unusual to be unable to get a ticket.

The film market is effectively divided into three. First there are the 200 or so screens in local cinemas, handling the mass-market products. It is these that have been most hit by closures, so that each suburban centre will now have one theatre at most. Some quite sizeable outer London shopping centres, like Twickenham, have no screens at all. Then there are the first-run cinemas in Park and City, many grouped around Leicester Square. Thirdly there are repertory and art theatres, catering for the film buff and the *aficionado* of foreign language films. Lost in the middle of all three sectors is the Israeli-owned Cannon chain, which has appeared from nowhere to challenge the dominance of Rank and EMI, the two main distributors. Cannon now have ten cinemas in central London, showing a curious mixture of suburban pap (sometimes bankrolled by the same company that owns the chain) and art films. The rumour is that Cannon will drive the diet of films in the central area downmarket. There is no clear sign of that happening yet, and at least Cannon cinemas are cheap.

No mention of London's cultural life would be complete without popular music. In my sample week, there were over 550 rock, folk and jazz gigs. The Friday, Saturday and Sunday nights of that week each offered a choice of 100 places to enjoy music. The scene has always been one that went in waves. The jazz clubs of the 1950s and early 1960s gave way to the pop music of the 1960s; then that gave way to the big glamorous concerts. Then, from the early 1970s on, an alternative music business grew up in the back rooms of pubs, like the Nashville on the Talgarth Road, The Greyhound in Fulham or the Hope & Anchor in Islington. But despite the happy memories that those in their late 30s have about pub-rock, it was never big business. There were far fewer gigs ten years ago than there are now.

What changed things? Punk, again. Don't fall for the line that punk was democratic art. As we have already seen, it wasn't; it came out of the art schools, just like many other British popular cultural movements. But it was easy art. It reclaimed from the expensive, light-showed concerts a sheer joy of making music scruffily. It spawned hundreds of new bands, and hundreds of new venues. And punk acted as a purgative on the system. Once it had cleaned everything out, all kinds of entertainment could colonise the new body musical. Post-punk music has included a revival of interest in jazz, which a decade ago was of very limited appeal, and even of folk music. Two of London's most popular bands in the past year – The Pogues and The Men They Couldn't Hang – have wedded punk to folk in a way that would have had the gentle purists of the 1960s burning their acoustic guitars. But then nobody in London is a purist any more; that's its joy.

In the decade since punk burst onto London's streets, the rock music business has demonstrated the purest form of entrepreneurialism in the capital. There have been some big operators – those who fill Wembley for Bruce Springsteen or The Police – but more interesting have been the small-timers who ran a couple of bands, organised a few venues, or designed a label or two. And they, too, have lived to learn that quality pays. Despite the wealth of available music, the audience is still discriminating, helped by a music press that is absurdly fervent in its likes and dislikes.

It wasn't just live music that punk encouraged. One of the more surprising developments in town in the late 1970s was the rediscovery of night-clubs – *Time Out* now regularly lists 70 each week. These range from crowded sweaty rooms playing a different kind of music every night, like the Sol y Sombra or the Wag Club, to established venues like Dingwall's at Camden Lock with live bands, to one of the many gay clubs, like Heaven, under the arches at the Embankment, to the little empire of Peter Stringfellow. He runs both an expensive, small night-club under his own name, and the Hippodrome (once the Talk of the Town) on Charing Cross Road. This is where the young workers from Bromley and Croydon descend on a Saturday night, marvelling at his light-show ("rumoured", people always say, "to have cost more than £1m"). It somehow isn't done to praise Mr Stringfellow, though I can't see why not. London ten years ago was a much too serious place, in which you were expected to talk about your day on the Grunwick picket line over a pint or four of real ale. What Stringfellow and his peers have done is to offer those kids who every summer enjoy sun and sex in Spain the equivalent in cold old London – glitter, cocktails, and a night full of West End promise.

Will those who have spent the last decade hoofing it round the new clubs graduate to the old ones; the expensive night-clubs and casinos of Mayfair? I doubt it. The new London night-life is democratic and domestic, the old class-ridden and foreign. Of course there have been exceptions, but I don't think that casinos, for example, have really made an impact on the average Londoner; they are for Arabs and Americans.

Above all, the scions of the new night-life have

succeeded in casting off an overt political stance while remaining altruistic. It would be wrong to use the word counter-culture about what's going on in London. There's nothing revolutionary about the people who enjoy its clubs and pubs, its rock music and its films, save that they are enjoying themselves in a culture that once looked as if it had forgotten the meaning of the term. Yet this same culture can be remarkably, spontaneously, generous. Nobody who saw young, hedonistic Britain's response to Band Aid/Live Aid/Fashion Aid and every other kind of Aid in 1985 could think that there was much wrong with the place. And the City? It failed to show any interest at all in a Bond Aid that some American brokers there proposed. If you want to find optimism about the future of London, and of Britain, follow the crowds to the Hippodrome or the Sol y Sombra.

Body and soul

Always, the maxim that quality pays is borne out. Take football. There are 12 professional football clubs in London; all of them have seen their attendances shrink dramatically since 1976. That in itself begs a question. There are understandable social reasons for thinking that football could never recapture the 80,000 crowds that some matches got immediately after the war. British society has become more affluent; more entertainment is available at home. Yet the gates continued to decline long after that affluence was established, and the reason must be that the clubs have not given potential spectators the quality of service that they deserve. Too many football grounds are, as a colleague of mine once astutely remarked, slum stadiums for slum people. In the wake of the Bradford fire disaster of 1985, one London ground, the Valley at Charlton, was found to be so unsafe that the club had to move. It now shares a ground with Crystal Palace.

I find this desperately sad, mainly because I think that

at its best football provides the closest thing to a regular
dose of beauty that anyone can afford. But I'm one of the
lost number. I always thought that no amount of scare
stories would put me off the occasional Saturday
afternoon at a game. One terrified hour at Stamford Bridge
in 1984 did. If you don't think that you're going to be safe
on the terraces, why risk your neck?

I could have been unlucky. I've never had any trouble
at Arsenal, say, which has nurtured a reputation as both a
well-run and well-policed club. But too many Saturdays
listening to the casual racism of the fans – still, despite
the evidence of how much young British blacks offer the
sport – has combined with the threat of violence to put
me and millions like me off. I want to be tempted back. I
remember how good football can be. I was standing in the
middle of a crush of Spurs supporters at Wembley when
Ricky Villa scored his winning goal in the 1981 Cup Final
replay. Life has offered few better things. But it will take a
lot to make me a regular again.

Should one watch rugby instead? No; it's not a
spectator sport in the same way, and though London fair
bristles with rugby clubs (a particular cluster of them
around the Upper Richmond Road), you have to play to
get the best out of rugby, or believe that the way to
recapture your lost youth is to sing songs in all-male
company and get drunk on too much beer. Cricket? I offer
the 1983 Benson & Hedges Final between Middlesex and
Essex as the most enjoyable purely London sporting event
I've ever seen. On a glorious summer's day, in from
Romford, Ilford and all the other townships of New Bow
Bells came the young cockneys to support Essex (most of
them stripped off bleached jeans halfway through the
afternoon to reveal satin shorts underneath). The
Middlesex supporters were a motley crew of old buffers
and young blacks – there's nothing quite like seeing a
Rastafarian selling programmes at Lord's. Everyone got
gently pissed together in the sun, and the match went to
the last over. Magic.

One could play football instead. Thousands do. Hackney Marshes from the air is a miracle – one pitch after another. Then there are the hard-surface, floodlit pitches where the local leagues meet, at Wormwood Scrubs, in the shadow of the prison, at Crystal Palace, or – a particularly nice one, with good views of the City – in Southwark Park. Others play cricket. You can still see village green cricket in London; try Twickenham, any Saturday or Sunday in the summer, and have a pint or two in the Prince Albert next to the green when you've had enough.

For those who regard themselves above team games, there is racket sport. The RAC club in Pall Mall at eight o'clock in the morning is full of American bankers looking as if they have just made a spectacular deal over a squash game. After they've outgrown squash, some whizzkids will pay a king's ransom for tennis. There's a set of indoor courts in Shepherd's Bush for which the membership fee and annual subscription is the best part of £1,000 – I think that's even more expensive than the Queen's Club, with its gorgeous pavilion stuck in the middle of Fulham.

Or you could dance. The high point of the aerobics craze seems to have passed, but some have made money from it. Again, Covent Garden led the way; the Pineapple Studios introduced dance as a keep-fit activity in London, though at least some of its fans must have promptly put on all the pounds they had lost in the Mexican restaurant next door. London has seen a crop of skiing shops too, and the air in Verbier and Val d'Isère (just "Val", to its British fans) crackles with Sloane Street accents every March. But appearances may deceive; when taxed, the owner of one of the new shops told me recently that the market for skiing was growing only slowly. He was relying on selling gear every winter to the same old customers rather than attracting new ones.

Church-going must count as another minority activity. *Faith in the City*, the 1986 report by the Church of

England, admitted that in many of Britain's inner cities –
including London – the church appealed to few. In
London, as elsewhere, it has been those churches that
have tried to maintain a traditional commitment to the
things of the soul that have done well. The black
churches in south London, full of revivalist fervour, have
been the most successful. St. James's, Piccadilly, has
cleverly combined a social function – it has a coffee shop,
lectures at lunchtime, and encourages strollers to use its
porch as a short-cut from Jermyn Street to Piccadilly –
with traditional services, and has done well on the
mixture. Elsewhere the picture is more disheartening.
According to Gavin Stamp in *The Spectator,* 124 Church
of England churches have closed in London since 1969.
Latest plans threaten some in the East End, including
Hawksmoor's incomparable St George-in-the-East.

From soul back to body. Where do Londoners find sex?
Not the red-light sex (that is in Soho, Shepherd Market – a
truly wonderful corner of London, just off Curzon Street –
or such seedy strips as Seven Sisters Road) but good
honest sex? It's much easier for gays. They head down the
Old Brompton Road to The Coleherne or Chaps, or to one
of the other pubs and clubs conveniently listed in *Time
Out* or *City Limits.* London has never had a truly
successful hetero singles-bar scene. In the early 1970s
some pubs on the King's Road came close; later, the wine
bars of Covent Garden did their bit. But too many women
friends tell me that there is an absence of non-seedy bars
where they might meet people – and many of my single
men friends agree. Sex in London still relies, I think, on
the great British party; the Saturday night thrash to which
everyone brings a bottle and the host or hostess makes
sure they've got plenty of salt (for red wine stains) and
enough Motown tapes to keep everyone happy. It's a
domestic kind of sex, really – but then for all the many
attractions of London, it has so many delightful places to
live that it remains, in large part, a stay-at-home,
domestic kind of town.

8
GOVERNING

They don't wear bowler hats any more, and they don't spend all their time drinking tea. They love the opera, and live in places like Strawberry Hill, Bromley, or Hampstead. A surprising number of the younger ones are women. The men get their suits and shirts from Marks & Spencer; they join the Wine Society, and throw parties where a Rolling Stones medley comes on at midnight. They prefer tennis to squash, and are mad about France. They read *The Times* (though they think its gone downhill) or *The Guardian,* and share the *Financial Times* in the office. They fight for the privilege of taking home the office copy of *The Economist* on a Friday evening. They complain about their pay – rightly – but remarkably few give up their hard job (they work very long hours) for the greener pastures of the City.

London is not a company town in the way that Washington and Canberra are. Millions of Londoners might know hardly anybody who works for the civil service or local government. Yet the business of oiling the wheels of government – Britain's government, not just London's – is one of the keys to understanding the city. Whitehall is where the governing takes place.

Whitehall is both a place and a frame of mind. The place is a street running gently downhill, north-south, from Trafalgar Square to Parliament Square. The state of mind is one that looks for order where there has been chaos, that values rationality and a calm approach, and which assumes that there is no problem that a bit of rule-making, a touch of precedent, some first-class minds,

and a *soupçon* of (strictly pin-striped) flair cannot solve.
Whitehall is not street-cred.

Whitehall the state of mind takes place in Whitehall the
place; and elsewhere. Britain's civil servants now work in
many places outside London. The Health & Safety
Executive is in Bootle, the Social Services' computer
centre in Newcastle, the Manpower Services Commission
in Sheffield – even the Royal Mint has left London for
Cardiff. Within London, Jobcentres, social security
offices, tax and customs offices and the like all employ
many thousands of people miles from Whitehall the
place. Indeed, the place no longer has all the
headquarters of the great ministries. The growth of
government since 1945 has long outstripped the capacity
of the street to cope.

The Inland Revenue has probably the finest government building of all – Somerset House, a Georgian palace
on the banks of the river (its terraces used to be lapped by
the water, before the Thames was trapped behind
strengthened banks) just west of Fleet Street. More modern
non-Whitehall headquarters buildings are less to write
home about. The Department of Health & Social Security
occupies two interlocking buildings at the Elephant &
Castle, a hideous road-junction-cum-shopping centre a
mile south of Westminster Bridge. The Department of
Trade & Industry is in two buildings along the dull
canyon of Victoria Street. Just to their south, in Marsham
Street, are the three 18-storey towers of the Departments
of Environment and Transport, which from all over
London look like a giant toast-rack. The Home Office,
evicted from Whitehall a decade ago, now occupies a
Lubianka overlooking St James's Park; the Department of
Employment, removed from elegant St James's Square a
little later, has a nearby office in Tothill Street. Perhaps
most awful of all this ugly bunch is the tower above
Waterloo Station, to which the Department of Education
was moved when the spooks of MI5 took over its Mayfair
offices in a building conspicuous by its anonymity.

Though thousands of civil servants no longer work there, Whitehall continues to give its name to the culture of the governing classes. Its equestrian statues, its horseguards, and the Cenotaph (the Edward Lutyens-designed memorial to the dead of the First World War) combine to give an air that is almost Parisian in its triumphalism, at least towards Parliament Square. The Trafalgar Square end is tacky, with souvenir stalls and the Whitehall Theatre, famous once for farces, then bought by Soho strip-club tycoon Paul Raymond, turned into a short-lived "Theatre of War", and now back in use as the real thing. From Great Scotland Yard the buildings start to impress. On the western side is the Old Admiralty Building, and facing it the Ministry of Agriculture and the Banqueting House. Back on the western side are the two delightful Georgian town houses now occupied, to the undisguised envy of the rest of the civil service, by the parliamentary counsel and the Scottish Office. The counsel, who draft the country's laws, are a collection of brilliant nit-pickers much given to the traditional gesture; they ceremonially take tea together every afternoon.

Across the way, guarded by a statue of Field-Marshal Montgomery (one of London's better modern statues) is the Ministry of Defence, a modern building which houses some 6,000 civil servants. Legend has it that it has as many floors below ground as above. I was once told that when you get to the bottom floors, below the level of the river, things are so damp that you have to wear Wellington boots all day, and that the only accents there are American. From the defence ministry to Parliament Square runs an undistinguished lot of nineteenth-century houses now given over to shops; they merge with others round the corner in Bridge Street. For longer than anyone cares to remember, plans have been afoot to turn this corner into decent offices for members of the House of Commons, who at present have to make do in one of a number of buildings scattered within running distance of the House.

Across the road from these shops stand the twin nineteenth-century buildings now occupied by the Treasury and the Foreign Office. The Treasury is remarkable. Four-square from the outside, on the inside it is constructed around a circle hidden in its middle. This gives lots of wide, curving corridors down which tea trolleys trundle, and into which Treasury men decamp to give voice to a madrigal or two. The corridors are almost oriental in their width and lightness, and it has been said that the building was really designed for the nineteenth-century Indian Civil Service in Bombay, and that the corridors were wide enough to have punkah-wallahs by the score. The plans got mixed up, apparently, and Bombay has our Treasury.

Next door, the Home Office used to share Sir Giles Gilbert Scott's government buildings with the Foreign Office, but the diplomats have got most of the building to themselves now. They are smooth, urbane men. Their next-door neighbours in the Treasury are hairy and tough. FO chaps slide under a door; Treasury men (and even more, Treasury women) kick it down. They do not like each other; the diplomats know that the Treasury is now top-dog, and so does the Treasury.

Just to the north of the Foreign Office is the epicentre of governing in Britain. Downing Street, a short cul-de-sac, runs into Whitehall from a terrace overlooking St James's Park. On its northern side stand Number 12 (the offices of the Government Whips), Number 11 (the home of the Chancellor of the Exchequer) and Number 10; these are the last of the eighteenth-century town houses left on the street. Number 10 has been the official residence of the Prime Minister since George II offered it to Walpole in 1732.

Number 10 is a most deceptive building. From the street it looks just like a fine London Georgian house. Look more closely; to its east, set back a little behind a patch called Treasury Green, is a quite substantial office block. This connects by means of a green baize door with the Old Treasury Building – now the Cabinet Office – on Whitehall. Together, Downing Street and the Cabinet Office form an L-shaped group within which the key government decisions of the day are taken. Neither is open to the public. This is a pity, for within the nineteenth-century shell of the Cabinet Office are some of London's most interesting Tudor remains, seen to their best advantage along Cockpit Passage, which runs from the front of the building to the back. At the north end of the building is a delightful set of Georgian rooms, now occupied by the Lord Privy Seal and Leader of the House of Commons.

Number 10 is a beautiful building, immaculately kept, and much bigger than most people guess. The Cabinet Room runs east-west on the ground floor, looking over Horse Guards Parade and St James's Park. The press office and the Prime Minister's private office are on that floor too, with the state entertaining rooms on the first floor (up a staircase lined with portraits of the house's occupants). The Prime Minister's personal quarters are under the eaves.

The Cabinet Office houses the Cabinet Secretariat, which co-ordinates all the business that comes before ministers for "collective decision" in cabinet or cabinet committee; a chunk of the Manpower & Personnel Office, which looks after the government machine itself; and, for le Carré fans, the offices of the Joint Intelligence Committee, on the second floor. Number 10 has the press office, into which troop, every morning, the journalists of the lobby, to be briefed on what the Prime Minister is up to. By the strange customs of the lobby, this meeting, vital to the public presentation of the government's position, does not take place at all, and the person from whom the briefing comes (one of the best known men in London) is known simply as "a source close to the Prime Minister".

Next to the press office is the Prime Minister's private office, made up of her Principal Private Secretary, who will usually be in his early 40s, and four bright young

civil servants – one for economic affairs, one for home
affairs, one for foreign affairs and defence, and one for
parliamentary matters. All five may be expected to get to
the top of their departments. All, of course, in the way of
the Whitehall system, are expected to be intensely loyal
to the Prime Minister while being perfectly prepared to
work under a chief of an opposing party the next day. The
Prime Minister has probably the smallest political office
of any western head of government and, on the upper
floors, a policy unit, full of bright young things who give
her one-side-of-a-piece-of-paper summaries of key issues.

A pagan place
Whitehall men and women are Londoners. They may not
hail from town – indeed, I think that less than a fair
proportion of them do – but they use it. They provide the
heart of the audience at the National Theatre, the
Barbican, the concert halls, and, especially, the opera. Sir
Robert Armstrong, the Head of the Civil Service, is also
Secretary of the board of the Royal Opera House, Covent
Garden; a visit to Glyndebourne is the kind of treat that
civil servants give themselves.

These most civilised of London's workers have to
co-exist with a small group of people whose tastes are less
refined. Like gentrifiers moving into a Brookstown
terrace, the denizens of Whitehall have to put up with the
rowdy, unreconstructed neighbours next door.

Every Tuesday and Thursday, the Prime Minister's
private office climb into their government-issue cars with
their chief and turn right out of Downing Street into
Whitehall. A couple of hundred yards later the cavalcade
enters Parliament Square, and then turns left into New
Palace Yard, the members' entrance to the House of
Commons.

The Commons, and its southerly neighbour the House
of Lords, together form a magnificent group of Victorian
perpendicular Gothic buildings, built to the designs of

Charles Barry between 1837 and 1860, after earlier buildings on the site (with the exception of the remarkable medieval Westminster Hall, with its famous hammerbeam roof) were burned down in 1834. Barry enlisted Augustus Pugin to decorate his new building, and Pugin ran riot. It is to him that we owe the wealth of detail of woodcut and stone carving that makes the Houses of Parliament so engaging. And now that the building has been cleaned, the full splendour of Barry's and Pugin's work can be seen to better effect than for a century.

These buildings inhabit the site of the old Westminster Palace, used by the first Norman kings. Westminster has been at the centre of the governing of the nation for nearly 1,000 years. It is national, and indeed international, affairs that exercise the minds of the 650 politicians in the House of Commons. They are not Londoners in the sense that Whitehall men and women are. Naturally, most of them live in London, at least during the week; you may find them in Eaton Square, or in the 1930s housing at Dolphin Square, or, increasingly, in Kennington and Vauxhall, south of Westminster Bridge. Many of them will have part-time jobs in London, particularly in the City or the Temple – lawyers have always been over-represented at Westminster – and 84 of them sit for London seats. But most MPs affect a suspicion of London. The true heart of the nation, they will always claim, is in their own constituency; in the villages of Suffolk Coastal, the working-men's clubs of Leeds West, the crofts of Caithness and Sutherland, the pits of Blaenau Gwent. London, they would have you believe, is meretricious, out-of-scale and corrupting.

These men – only a handful of women – provide, on occasion, London's greatest theatre. Forget the claims that parliament is not what it was, and that it does not control the executive. A great day in the House of Commons can provide a buzz of excitement which no legislature in the world can rival. Any person who wants to capture some of London's most vivid colour should get to at least one grand occasion in the House. I shall never forget the debate in January, 1986 on the Prime Minister's handling of the Westland crisis. Mrs Thatcher and Neil Kinnock, the leader of the Labour Party, were just a warm-up act. David Owen, the leader of the Social Democrats, spoke for ten minutes without a note, leaning forward so that one felt that he was about to touch the Prime Minister, and never taking his eyes off her. Michael Heseltine, who had precipitated the crisis, spoke of his loyalty to party and Prime Minister; Michael Foot reminded him that "you can rat; but you can't re-rat". In the press gallery, over a hundred journalists sat spellbound, then hurried to their 'phones, and the bars to discuss who had done well in a performance that Dickens – a parliamentary sketch-writer of distinction – would have recognised instantly.

Outside the chamber, in the lobbies, journalists beard members for off-the-record briefings. It was here, in 1948, that Hugh Dalton let slip a budget secret to a journalist minutes before his speech. The journalist's son, Robert Carvel of the *Evening Standard,* was standing there listening; he is now the doyen of the press gallery, and in that wonderfully parliamentary sense of tradition, his own son, John, is *The Guardian*'s House of Commons man. He and his colleagues may be seen hanging around in the long committee corridor which runs the length of the Palace, waiting for a story, or, in summer, drinking on the terrace, or popping into the red-leathered splendour of the House of Lords, one of my candidates for the finest room in Christendom.

Westminster is a magic place; but a pagan place too, full of pomposity and dirty deeds. This is where the knives go in; this is where reputations are lost over a bottle of claret. It is a self-enclosed world, one whose values are not those of the city or country outside. It is a place of honour and dishonour, of boredom and quick excitement, of late-night sessions when the House is deserted and great occasions when it cannot seat all those who want to get in. It is a place of self-importance; which perhaps explains why those who work there have, in the main, had little time for the inhabitants of the building that lies across the river from Westminster, challenging it like a spaniel might snap at a duke's ankles.

The end of an alternative

County Hall was built between 1909 and 1933 to the design of Ralph Knott. It occupies a marvellous position on the South Bank, just to the north of Westminster Bridge. From 1922 (when its first sections were opened) until 1965, it was the home of the London County Council; from then until 1986 it housed the GLC. For a brief time in the early 1980s, the goings-on within its Italianate courtyards of Portland stone almost rivalled the House of Commons for passion and derring-do.

Britain is not the only country to have had trouble with the government of its capital city. Remember the Paris Commune; remember that until 1974 Washington, DC was run by Congress, not by an elected authority. From the point of view of the national government, London has always been a source of potential problems. Charles I found that London would provide a haven for those parliamentarians whom he wanted locked up; London yelled "Wilkes and Liberty" when Georgian governments wanted to shackle both; Londoners supported the General Strike of 1926. If the story of London's government from 1981 to 1986 lacks this sense of colour and risk, it is nonetheless essential to an understanding of the modern city.

The GLC was only created in 1963. In the fashion of those days, it was meant to be a "strategic" authority. It would have control of major issues of land-use and development, manage the old LCC housing estates (though it was expected to hand them over to the boroughs), supervise major roads, fund London Transport, and, through a sub-committee, run education in the old LCC area of inner London. For 16 years it struggled to find a role; when that role was discovered in 1981, it was not one that was likely to endear it to either party in the House of Commons.

Mrs Thatcher had won a landslide victory in the general election of 1979. Between then and 1981 the Labour Party had torn itself apart. It split into the old party faithfuls, who favoured moderate, throw-money-at-it corporatism, and a younger, much more radical wing. Labour won the 1981 GLC elections. Within a day, the moderate leadership had been pushed out. Young Turks led by Ken Livingstone took over. They then consciously threw down a gauntlet. The capital was to be the test bed for a new kind of politics; one that would challenge both the Conservative central government and the Whitehall-knows-best style of the old Labour Party.

County Hall was thrown open to the public. It hummed with meetings as the new GLC invited representatives of those groups on whom it wanted to spend time and money; blacks, Irish, women, the young – anyone who had been marginalised by traditional, big-battalion politics. Soon, lots of these groups were receiving grants from the GLC's ever-open coffers. At the same time, Livingstone and his deputies determined to slash the fares on London Transport, and appeared to look more favourably on the IRA (who for ten years had carried on a sporadic bombing campaign in the capital) than they did on the Metropolitan Police.

To the Conservatives, the challenge that Livingstone threw down was essentially an economic one. Previous GLC administrations had never had much of an economic policy. Livingstone and his lieutenant Mike Ward did; they set up the Greater London Enterprise Board (GLEB) to prove to the free-market Thatcher government that public intervention in the economy could bring new jobs to the city. To Labour, the challenge was to take seriously groups other than the trade-union-organised, white working-class on which the party had relied for support.

Livingstone understood that that class had both shrunk and changed. If Labour was to be relevant, it had to reach out to those whom politics had left behind.

Within months, Livingstone's rent-a-quote politics had made him the right-wing media's main hate figure – and not just with the Conservatives. In 1982 the Bermondsey Labour Party, in the heart of declining dockland, had to select a new candidate for its parliamentary seat. Bob Mellish, the sitting member, had had enough of the parliamentary game, and was leaving to become deputy chairman of the LDDC. Mellish was the apotheosis of the old, right-wing, manual worker-based London Labour Party – a bit of a thug with a heart of gold. He had not changed since he first came into politics. That meant that by 1982 he had become utterly out of touch with the young left-wingers who ran his party. They chose one of their own number, Peter Tatchell, as the candidate.

Tatchell looked an identikit member of the Livingstone-era GLC. Gay, young, a community worker, middle-class but living in a council block, he epitomised radical chic. The Labour party nationally tried and failed to block his nomination. When the by-election took place in early 1983, Simon Hughes stole for the Liberals (and held in the general election) a seat that by every demographic indicator should be solidly Labour. It was not the kind of performance that was likely to endear the new London Labour Party to the *apparatchiks* in Westminster.

The Tatchell story was followed closely – perhaps too closely – by Mrs Thatcher and her ministers. They had been appalled by the chaos that followed from Bromley council's successful legal challenge to the GLC's fare cuts in 1982, and had started to think about removing London Transport from the GLC's grasp. But if the London Labour Party was so unpopular, might this not be the right time to complete the business left unfinished in 1965? If the GLC was both troublesome and short of support (and so it looked in 1982 and early 1983), why not abolish this costly tier of government and return all power to the boroughs?

Of all the many myths that surround the story of the abolition of the GLC, none is more fervently believed than that Mrs Thatcher personally inserted the abolition plan into the Conservatives' manifesto for the 1983 general election at the last minute. This is not so. Plenty of suburban Tory politicians had been keen to get rid of the GLC since 1965. They did not like paying for its airs and graces, and bitterly resented its efforts to get them to share the problems of the inner city. Some Whitehall officials had marked the GLC's card ever since the Ringway fiasco. Mrs Thatcher's cabinet started considering abolition in the summer of 1982; first proposals to that effect were brought forward by Michael Heseltine, Secretary of State for the Environment, whom supporters of the GLC were later to claim had been on their side all along. By Christmas, 1982, the GLC's fate had been decided; not a single cabinet minister had opposed the plan. The commitment to abolition in the manifesto was merely the first public sign of a cabinet decision that had been taken months before.

But what had seemed such a good idea in 1982 was much less of a winner in late 1983. With all the fickleness of which it is a master, the press suddenly decided that Livingstone was not so much a mad Commie as a lovable rogue. There he was, living in his bedsit with his salamanders, travelling to work by public transport, refusing to put on the know-it-all style of politicians – why, he was almost human! Moreover, given the scale of Mrs Thatcher's victory in 1983, the Labour Party nationally had to find an issue, quickly, on which it could hit back at the Conservatives. It found it in the abolition of the GLC; this, it said, would leave administration in London in a shambles, and was, in any event, undemocratic. The GLC helped keep the show on the road with a brilliant series of advertisements based on the theme "Say no to no say".

With the carelessness that it brought to many decisions
after the 1983 triumph, the government then compound-
ed the felony. The new Secretary of State for the
Environment, Patrick Jenkin, had none of Heseltine's
sharpness. He was meat and drink to a savvy, street-wise
politician like Livingstone. Jenkin's first decision was a
disaster. Abolition had not been properly thought
through in Whitehall, which meant that it had to be
effected by two Acts of Parliament, not one. The GLC
would thus have to be tolerated for nearly three years,
until the spring of 1986. But what to do with the GLC
elections in 1985? All members of the government were
agreed that these could not go ahead, because Livingstone
would turn them into a referendum on abolition – and in
the middle of a parliament, he would probably win. The
Prime Minister suggested that the GLC elected in 1981
should have its life extended for a year without new
elections. Jenkin disagreed, and convinced the Cabinet to
scrap the elections, remove the 1981 class of councillors
in 1985, and run the GLC for its last year by an appointed
body drawn from the boroughs – on which the
Conservatives would have a majority.

This was the decision which finished Jenkin's political
career. It was presented by Labour as a blatant attempt to
change the political complexion of an elected body by
administrative fiat. Tories opposed to Mrs Thatcher's
style rallied to the defence of democracy and in summer,
1984, the House of Lords junked the Jenkin package. The
1981 councillors thus held their seats until 1986.

Livingstone had made all the running since the general
election of 1983. Opinion polls said that 84% of all
Londoners wanted an elected, city-wide authority. The
government's response, in September, 1984, was to
augment Jenkin's team at the Department of the
Environment. Kenneth Baker was moved from his job as
minister for new technology to be Jenkin's number two.
He had once sat for a London parliamentary seat, and
knew all about London government – indeed, he had at

one time written a pamphlet defending the GLC. At last, the Tories had found a match for Livingstone's propaganda. From the moment of Baker's appointment, the battle started to go the government's way. The abolition bill was passed in summer, 1985, the heart went out of County Hall, Livingstone got adopted for a parliamentary seat in Brent, Jenkin got sacked and was replaced by Baker, and at midnight on March 31st 1986, 97 years of London-wide government came to an end.

In Chapter 9 we shall look again at life without the GLC. But whether or not London can exist without a city-wide body is not the real message of what must now be known as the Livingstone years. What this curiously uncharismatic, low-key, slightly podgy, man did was to make politics in London both dangerous and fun. Some of those allied to Livingstone were unscrupulous in the use of power. They handed out grants to their supporters, they backed some crazy ideas, they encouraged some politicians way to the left of them to believe that anything was possible – and some of the left in London lack even an ounce of Livingstone's undoubted charm. They don't show much consistency either. In the spring of 1985, the Labour group on the GLC split asunder when the hard left refused to set a rate for the coming financial year. Livingstone and his chairman of finance, John McDonnell, fell out amid bitter recriminations and accusations of a sell-out to the Tories. The GLC was dangerous, too, because it simply lacked the competence necessary to carry out its more grandiose plans. Much of the good work of the Greater London Enterprise Board, for example, had the gloss taken off it when it was revealed that some schemes had been approved without proper consideration, and quite substantial sums of public money lost.

It was, and remains, easy to have a laugh at some of the schemes and groups that the GLC backed. Yet it *was* important to support the women's movement, it *was* important to support blacks, it *was* important to convince the Irish community that they had a role in London, it *was* important to get bike-lanes through the streets, it *was* important to cut public transport fares, it was important to go all-out for cultural politics. It was Livingstone's GLC that introduced Thamesday, a day's worth of fun on the river, his administration that opened up the South Bank arts complex to more popular shows, his officers that backed rock and jazz festivals.

This may not be the stuff of high politics, but they were the kind of things to which ordinary Londoners wanted to see their hitherto self-important politicians devote time and effort. Livingstone was never street-cred – he is an intensely political person, and street-cred is sceptical of such commitment. But plenty of the things he did went with the grain of the street-cred economy. He once told me that he was all in favour of an entrepreneurial culture, so long as minimum standards of employment and protection and safety were guaranteed. On balance, I believe him. He understood the new London, in all its quirky creativity, better than any other politician. He spoke the language of young Londoners, and they in their turn responded by supporting his campaign to save the GLC. In 1985, he won the ultimate accolade. After two near-misses, he came top of the *City Limits* poll for "the person you would most like to spend an afternoon on Clapham Common with". Some of the creative, slightly radical people on whom London's future largely depends would think that quite a compliment.

Rotten?

What of the boroughs, the 32 public authorities who will take over many of the GLC's functions? These divide naturally into the inner 12, with jurisdiction over an area close to this book's regions of Park and City, Brookstown, Crescent and Micawber, and an outer 20. There are three obvious differences between them. The outer boroughs are richer, more likely to vote Tory, and run their own

education services – the inner 12 are grouped together
into the Inner London Education Authority, known as the
ILEA.

The population of Greater London on census night,
1961 was very nearly 8m, which would have given an
average borough size of 250,000. That was the figure that
most assumed each borough would have. But things have
not worked out like that. At the 1981 census, Croydon,
the most populous borough, had 317,000, only a little
below its population in 1961 (it is now probably up to the
level it was then). Bexley, Bromley, Hillingdon and
Sutton – all in the outer 20 – each had more people in
1981 than in 1961. By contrast, in those 20 years, both
Islington and Southwark lost 100,000 people; all told, the
inner 12 lost 900,000 people, the outer 20 only about
300,000. Three inner London boroughs – Hammersmith &
Fulham, Tower Hamlets and Kensington & Chelsea – now
have populations of under 150,000, as does one outer
borough, Kingston.

The flight of population from inner London has left the
12 boroughs facing enormous problems. Those who
are left tend to be older or younger, are more often
unemployed, and are more likely to live in council
housing. They are thus net consumers of public services;
but of course the decline in population means that their
consumption has to be funded by a shrinking tax base.
That is one reason why, despite much distrust (of which
more later), successive Conservative governments have
never been able to bring themselves to abolish the ILEA. If
the costs and management problems of education were
heaped onto the individual inner boroughs, some of them
would simply be unable to cope.

These inner 12 boroughs have always tended to be
Labour-controlled, but the decline of the old working-
class, moderate Labour Party and its replacement by a
more radical variant has taken different forms in different
boroughs. In Tower Hamlets, for example, some of the old
spirit lives on, disastrously. The main opposition to the

Labour old guard there comes from a radical Liberal Party. In the two boroughs of Camden and Islington, which both have a mix of the social characteristics of Brookstown and Crescent, the young, professional, graduate Labour Party is strong. Frank Dobson, now Labour's shadow spokesman for health in the House of Commons was a Camden councillor; Jeremy Corbyn, Labour MP for North Islington, cut his teeth by opposing the widening of the Archway Road in the early 1970s. In a typical north Brookstown touch, the first member of parliament to publicly declare himself gay was Chris Smith, the excellent Labour MP for Islington South and Finsbury. Throughout Islington, the old, often Irish, right-wing Mafia deserted *en bloc* to the Social Democrats in 1981, and promptly lost their seats to the younger crowd. Islington is now led by Margaret Hodge, a rich, sensible, left-wing socialist who is turning into one of London's most influential politicians.

In 1984 and 1985, Hackney had three leaders of its council in 18 months, as different factions in the Labour group fought for control. One council meeting there in 1985 broke up in a public brawl. Similar behaviour has been seen south of the river. Southwark has had periods when it was effectively run by a committee of shop stewards from its trade unions; for the last few years Lambeth has been run by an uneasy coalition of radical blacks from Brixton and the hardest of London Labour's hard left. Council leader Ted Knight epitomised its uncompromising nature. He had been a long-standing ally of Ken Livingstone, but fell out with him during the left's great crisis over the setting of a GLC rate in 1985. The hard left refused to set a rate in line with the government's rate-capping laws. Livingstone and a majority of the GLC Labour group thought this was unrealistic. Knight delayed setting Lambeth's rate, and made common cause with John McDonnell, who had been Livingstone's deputy. Not that it did him much good. By March, 1986, the delay in Lambeth had been used by the district auditor as a rod to beat Knight with. Along with his colleagues on the Labour group at Lambeth, he was surcharged and banned from public office for five years.

In general, London's Tories have never been so colourful, though Sir Horace Cutler, who led the GLC before Livingstone, was something of an old-fashioned card. The most interesting of the modern Tories – if she can hold on to her power base at Westminster council – is Lady Porter. Shirley Porter is the daughter of Lord Cohen, the founder of Tesco supermarkets, and the husband of its managing director. She is a wonderfully feisty lady who would be at home in the rough, tumble and showmanship of American politics. During the campaign to abolish the GLC she never wavered from the government's line – unlike some of her colleagues on the wetter reaches of the Tory party, some of whom openly rebelled against Mrs Thatcher's plans.

If she continues in her position as leader of Westminster, Shirley Porter will become Mrs London; for in the absence of the GLC, Westminster will increasingly be looked to as the spokesman for all of central London. I suspect that she has territorial ambitions. She is not the only Conservative politician to have noticed that the boroughs are smaller than they were intended to be 20 years ago, but she is the only one with the *chutzpah* to do something about it. If the Secretary of State for the Environment decides, within the next few years, to amalgamate some boroughs (a scenario we will examine more closely in Chapter 9), then Lady Porter is likely to convince him that Westminster should be allowed to grow. It might, for example, merge with both Kensington & Chelsea and with Camden to provide one political unit for the geographical district of Park and City.

Most of the outer 20 boroughs have tended to support the Conservatives – but not Newham, which is an inner London borough in all but name, and not always Brent, where the political forces are evenly balanced. Haringey (which with Brent and Newham forms an uneasy threesome of "inner-outer boroughs") has a Labour Party almost as left-wing as Lambeth's. Between 1983 and 1986, its moderate councillors were elbowed out of the way, and its leadership was grabbed by Bernie Grant, one of the handful of blacks selected to fight a winnable Labour seat at the next general election. Grant became the media's pet hate in 1985 when he said that the police had got "a bloody good hiding" at Broadwater Farm. It was not a clever remark, yet it should not be thought either that it defines the man (he unquestionably has the interests of Haringey at heart) or that it was out of keeping with the mood of young blacks in Tottenham. Certainly, Grant had to face a protest march by his white council-workers who were rightly outraged by his insensitivity; at the same time, his unequivocal conde- mnation of police action made him, for a while, the most popular politician among the country's black population.

Richmond is a political oddity. It has two-party politics, but of a peculiar kind, for the Liberal Party has succeeded in ousting Labour from the council chamber entirely. Conservatives and Liberals divide the political spoils almost equally. Richmond Liberals are an interesting bunch, and the kind that the rest of their slightly chaotic party could learn from. Though they do lots of doorstep cleaning, leafleting, and all the rest of the community politics that the Liberals are famous for, they are led by a bunch of hard-nosed professionals, and have used modern management techniques to ensure that services are delivered in as cost-effective a way as possible.

The kids are all right, maybe

In all the outer 20 boroughs the key political issue is education. They are their own education authorities, whereas the ILEA runs the education service for the inner 12. This means that in inner London housing tends to be the issue that most concerns the boroughs. The problem for the outer 20 is that they are pretty small to be fully-fledged education authorities. Most people in Britain, let alone outside it, do not realise how big their units of local government are. Essex, Kent and Hampshire, for instance, each with a population of more than 1m, are bigger than 16 American states. Some of the outer London boroughs are tiny by comparison. Kingston has had real problems financing the polytechnic within its boundaries; both Sutton and Haringey have received highly critical reports from Her Majesty's Inspectors of Schools.

If the outer boroughs are too small to guarantee an education service of comprehensive excellence, there are those who would argue that the ILEA is too big. It costs something like £1 billion a year to run, has nearly 1,000 schools, over 250,000 pupils, 20,000 teachers, 34 colleges of further education, and supports five polytechnics. It is usually described (though I have never been able to hunt down the figures on which the claim is based) to be the biggest locally run education authority in the world.

It certainly has some of the world's greatest problems. The population of inner London has declined. So has the birth rate, all over Britain. Thus the ILEA is about two-thirds through a ten-year cycle which will see its school rolls decline from 333,000 primary and secondary school pupils in 1979 to only 248,000 in 1989 – a drop of 25%. Many of those left in inner London are poor; those middle-class parents who remain tend increasingly to educate their children privately. Thus in 1984 (the last year for which figures are available) 44.5% of primary school children had parents who were poor enough for their children to qualify for free school meals; the same applied to 40% of secondary school pupils. In some areas the figures were frightening. In Tower Hamlets, for example, no less than two out of every three pupils get free school meals.

Add to this crude measure of social deprivation among

the ILEA's intake three other factors. A quarter of all
children in the system come from single-parent families
(about 30% in Hackney). It is impossible to meet a
thoughtful teacher who denies that the scale of a school's
problems is not directly related to the number of children
in it from broken homes. Second, the ILEA has to teach
over 50,000 children whose mother tongue is not English.
At the last count, there were 147 languages spoken by
ILEA children – Bengali was the most common (used by
18% of those who spoke a foreign language). Urdu,
Gujarati and Punjabi made up another 19%. In 1983, 13%
of all primary school pupils were not fluent in English.

The third factor is a corollary of the second. The ILEA
classifies all its pupils by ethnic groups. In 1983-84, only
56% of primary school pupils and 61% of those in
secondary schools were classified as coming from the
British Isles; in Hackney, only 40%. Nearly 40% of Tower
Hamlets' primary school children were Bangladeshi; 30%
of Lambeth's secondary school pupils were classified as
Caribbean.

It would need a regiment of saints to administer such a
diverse brood so that they all got the education they
deserve. In its more than 20-year history, the ILEA has not
been short of boosters who have claimed that, against all
odds, it has managed to pull the trick off. Some of its
achievements have undoubtedly been not just praisewor-
thy but excellent. Many of its primary schools are
first-class; its non-mother tongue teaching is good; it has
taken further education seriously; its worst critics would
not deny that its provision for those with special
educational needs has been exemplary; its research
department has acted as a resource for the whole of the
British educational system. There was a time, in the
mid-1960s, when the ILEA was the trendy thing to
support: Holland Park and Pimlico secondary schools
were more fashionable than Eton.

Yet there has always been something fishy about the
backing that the ILEA has had. It was, in large measure,

the creation of civil servants in the Department of Education. They persuaded their ministers in the early 1960s that, however the government of London might be reformed, its inner city needed a unitary education authority. There is a strong case for arguing that for many years those officials were unwilling or unable to recognise the blemishes in their favourite son. Moreover, the ILEA is governed (with some additions from co-optees and representatives from the outer 20) by councillors elected to the GLC by the inner 12 boroughs. These have been overwhelmingly Labour. Thus the ILEA came to replace the old LCC as the jewel in Labour's local government crown. Any criticism of it was dismissed as motivated by baseless political considerations.

These defenders of the ILEA no longer make common ground. Many Conservative politicians (including the Prime Minister, whose *bête noire* the ILEA was when she was Minister for Education) have long believed that education in inner London was in the hands of mad left-wingers who were subverting the minds of children. Gradually, the Department of Education has had to take account of this view. It has succeeded, so far, in heading off continuing Conservative pressure for the break-up of the ILEA, but is now much more willing to criticise the Authority over, for example, its non-teaching costs. These are significantly higher than those in comparable cities. This criticism of the ILEA has reinforced the Labour Party's defensiveness. Since Mrs Frances Morrell took over the chair of the ILEA committee in 1983, the Authority has, in the eyes of its critics, aggressively pursued egalitarian policies – and more. There are those who have criticised the ILEA for the emphasis that it has placed on eradicating racism in the schools (a stupid objection), and others who argue that ILEA policies deprecating competitive sport are just silly. Underlying all these grievances is the claim that children from ILEA schools under-achieve. Figures published in 1984 on the performance of children in examinations ranked the ILEA

91st out of the 96 education authorities in England.

Yet things are never that simple. When social background of children was allowed for, those same figures showed that the ILEA's performance was much better than the crude figures suggested – it leapt to 45th place. And who would seriously argue that performance in examinations is the only indicator against which a school system should be measured? In reality, the ILEA is a curate's egg, and it would be most surprising if it was anything else. It has some bad schools, and almost certainly has more than its fair share of poor quality teachers, recruited into the profession in the early 1960s. Moreover, some of those teachers are so politically motivated that their ability to provide an unbiased, high-quality education is impaired. Some of them would openly regard that as an elitist goal, or one that merely provided fodder for the grinding mills of capitalism. The Inner London Teachers' Association is one of the most militant unions in the country. Yet for all those black marks, the fact remains that ILEA administrators are aware of the problems of their Authority, would like to improve it, and have to run an education service with more problems than anyone could reasonably land on people. They have to work for a highly politicised Authority, with an equally highly politicised and oppositely-inclined central government breathing down their necks.

The greatest challenge facing the Authority now is that many parents – white middle-class, and, increasingly, black working-class – are simply not prepared to accept the balanced view of the ILEA put forward here. They are voting with their feet. That can mean searching high and low for a church school for primary children – I wait for research that proves that attendance at the local Anglican church in inner London is directly correlated to the need to get a certificate of entry to a church school from the vicar – or, for black parents, placing children into one of the traditionally-taught black schools now springing up.

That solves the primary problem; at secondary level, the answer for those who can afford it is straightforward – pay for private education. Once London dinner-parties have exhausted house prices as a topic of conversation, they move on to the cost of schooling. One couple will be putting their children down for Latymer, another for Westminster, another for St Paul's. Then the local stalwart of the Labour Party will explode that there is no hope of improving the quality of ILEA schools if the middle-class desert them, and then the guilty parties reply (on the third bottle of Rioja) that that may be fine in theory, but I'm not sacrificing my children for a political principle, thank you very much.

And of course everyone is right. The Labour Party stalwart is right because the flight of the middle-class will leave – is already leaving – sink schools drawing their children from sink housing-estates. That way lies the dangerous prospect of the alienation of inner-city children. And the guilty parents are right, because why, indeed, should they sacrifice their children to teachers who will not unlock their potential? The great tragedy of education in inner London is that – with the very limited exception of Church of England primary schools – it lacks any organisation that can play the vital role that housing associations play in the housing field. Wanted: private money, charitable endowments, co-operatively and parent-run schools that can compete with each other for excellence and provide a diversity of education which extends, not just to those who can buy good schools and teachers for their children, but to those who, hitherto, have been too poor to afford that escape.

Another kind of School
Though the ILEA has some control over the London polytechnics, in practice they have substantial freedom over the way they conduct their academic affairs. At their best – as in the City Poly, which has played a valuable

role in providing qualifications for all kinds of workers in the Square Mile – they are at least of the same quality as many universities. Others have had less happy histories; the Polytechnic of North London, for example, had continuous trouble through the early 1970s when some left-wing staff and students had a series of rows with a more traditional director.

The University of London has never been under local government control. "The University" itself is something of a misnomer; it consists, to all intents and purposes, solely of Senate House, the strange Stalinist building in Bloomsbury which houses the administration for a federal collection of colleges, each of which is a mini-university in its own right. The last five years has seen a rationalisation of the colleges in the face of severe financial constraints. Small colleges have merged either with each other (as in the case of Bedford and Royal Holloway) or with bigger ones (Chelsea College, for example, has been taken over by King's). Increasingly, the power of the university has come to be concentrated on four centres of excellence.

The first of these, University College, was founded in 1826 to offer university education to those who were not communicants of the Church of England, and thus could not attend Oxford or Cambridge. It occupies splendid classical buildings on Gower Street, but the tightness of the development in that part of London means that it is now almost impossible to see the college as it was originally designed. Jeremy Bentham, the philosopher, was intimately connected with it in its early years, and left his body to the college – he may be seen, stuffed, wearing a battered old hat, his hand resting on a cane, on the first-floor landing. King's College was established two years after University College as a "Godly" rival, and still teaches theology. Like University College, its buildings, next to Somerset House, can no longer be appreciated for the grand design they were. Imperial, founded in 1907, forms part of the marvellous collection of Victorian and

Edwardian architecture in Kensington. Appropriately for a college so close to the Natural History and Science Museums, it has always concentrated on the natural sciences and technology.

And then there is the London School of Economics & Political Science – the LSE. Though a fully-fledged part of the university, "the School", as its people always describe it, takes a more than slightly sniffy attitude to the other colleges and to Senate House. Founded in 1895 by some early Fabians, including the Webbs (of whom the school has a good painting) and George Bernard Shaw, it is a most peculiar place. Uniquely for British universities, it concentrates on the social sciences, has about half its students taking post-graduate degrees, and has always drawn roughly half its students from abroad. Its buildings are hideously overcrowded – it would be a great mistake to go to the LSE for a sylvan campus, seeing as the only spot of open air is to be found on a roof-terrace, constantly littered with polystyrene cups.

Both because so many foreign politicians graduated from the LSE, and because it has always had a high-quality economics faculty, the School's reputation outside Britain has been secure. Its current director is an Indian economist, and his immediate predecessor was a German sociologist, Ralf Dahrendorf. Yet within Britain the LSE has never had an easy time. In the 1930s it was thought to be inhabited by rather sexless, earnest young men and women. Then, after the war, it was automatically associated with Harold Laski, a leading left-wing intellectual of the day. In 1968 it was the only place in Britain that exhibited the kind of student radicalism of the Sorbonne and Berkeley. For a while the School had to be closed, and to this day there are splits in the senior common room depending on which side of its glass doors one was when the barricades went up. All this has given it a reputation as a hot-bed of left-wing, revolutionary thought.

Nothing could be further from the truth. One

long-standing professor (who knew a thing or two about elections) used to claim that the senior common room had voted Tory at every chance since 1945. Its economic faculty has boasted such free-market theorists as Hayek; Karl Popper, the intellectual scourge of Marxism, taught at the School for many years, and its students have tended since the heady days of the 1960s to be interested less in revolution and more in making successful careers in the City or the law. Its cosmopolitan air was threatened by the ending of subsidised fees for foreign students in 1980, but the School responded, under Dahrendorf's direction, by going entrepreneurial. Teams were sent to the USA to recruit young Americans, who now fill the place to bursting point – wondering, sometimes, quite how this shambolic place could have got such plaudits from their professors back home.

On balance, it deserves them. Though some of its teachers too often give the impression that students get in the way of what a university is really about, at its best it provides a lively atmopshere that is refreshingly free of the intellectual isolation of many British universities. Perched on the edge of Fleet Street, and a short walk from Whitehall and Westminster, in any week the LSE provides fare from anyone in London worth their salt. Politicians and commentators drop in – there is a story that Attlee gave classes while still prime minister. I think of it as nothing less than the intellectual heart of the city – and if you're wondering, yes, I *am* biased; I spent five years teaching there, tucked away in a cubby-hole of a room facing a brick wall, and still on occasion miss the old place.

Not healthy
The National Health Service (NHS) in London is administered by health authorities – four regional authorities, each of which stretches well into the suburbs, and more than a hundred district authorities. For 18

years, between 1930 and 1948, the LCC was a health authority in its own right, with over 100 hospitals and more than 70,000 beds. That empire was lost with the coming of the NHS.

Health care in London has always been bifocated. The city has a concentration of great teaching hospitals, some of them, like Guy's, founded in 1721, of great antiquity. At the same time, it has traditionally had a lot of single-handed general practices with small lists and patchy primary care. The shrinking of the population has placed a strain on the teaching hospitals, which no longer have the quantity of patients that they were set up to cope with. Some have merged – Westminster Hospital Medical School, for example, is now located in the soulless skyscraper of the Charing Cross Hospital (which is in Hammersmith, not at Charing Cross). Complicated systems for allocating resources among the country's regions have tended to benefit the rest of the country and hit London. Many small hospitals have been closed – in 1968 London had 357 hospitals, in 1984 only 230 – and some of those left have had to cut their coats to a very tight financial cloth.

Though to a lesser extent, the same tensions which are clear in education affect London's health care too. The wealth of London's population relative to the rest of the country means that proportionately more Londoners get their health care from outside the NHS. In 1983, for example, the four regional authorities covering London had 40% of all the private beds in England. Like most issues in London, health has become politicised. The closure and merger of some medical schools was fought bitterly. The NHS is the largest single employer in the city, with over 130,000 workers, and unions have always been strong among its scandalously poorly-paid, often black, ancillary workers. Campaigns like the movement for natural childbirth have been focused on London; the great champion of the cause, Dr Wendy Savage, practised at The London Hospital. Yet without the focus of an elected local authority which looks after health care, the political issues usually lack the immediacy and local colour of those in education and housing. It is only in the last year that cuts in health provision have captured the public imagination, but a meeting of the West Lambeth Authority this year that was subject to much heckling may presage a new style. Hitherto, like most Britons (but with less justification) Londoners have regarded the problems of the health service as raising questions for national rather than local resolution.

They have not taken that view of the Metropolitan Police — "the Met", to all Londoners — whose 27,000 officers account for roughly a quarter of the country's police establishment. Of all the problems regarding the way in which London should be governed in the twenty-first century, none is so important or difficult to get right as the relationship between London's police and its people.

The importance of that relationship does not lie solely in the crime figures – though those are worrying. In 1974 there were 414,000 recorded offences in the Met's area (which extends a little beyond the 32 boroughs, and excludes the City). In 1984 there were 717,000, a rise of 73%. By contrast, whereas in 1974 27.5% of those offences were cleared up, in 1984 only 17% were; that is a measure of performance that does not suggest that all is well with the police. Crimes of violence have risen alarmingly. In 1974, 9,600 of them were recorded; in 1984, 19,000, an increase of 98%. Street robbery of personal property – mugging – increased in the decade by over 400%.

These figures are frightening. They are rendered more frightening still by a breakdown in relationships of trust between significant sections of London's population and the Met. There is nothing new in this. Forget, for the moment, the image of the bobby on the beat, supported by a grateful populace, his face stoic in the light shed by a blue lamp outside his station. Sir Robert Peel's force was unpopular from its foundation in 1829. Riots against the police were a regular feature of the nineteenth century (in one early one, the death of a policeman by stabbing was called "justifiable homicide" by a jury. Corruption and strikes periodically sullied the image of the force. Not until the 1940s and 1950s could it honestly be said that the Met had a good name.

It didn't last. At the end of the 1960s, the exposure of widespread corruption in the Met damaged public confidence once more; in the 1970s the force became the target for attacks from the left, and to some extent, from the apolitical middle-class. In 1979, a young New Zealander, Blair Peach, was killed, almost certainly by the police, during a demonstration in Southall. Nobody has ever been brought to book for his death.

The 1980s brought new tensions, or rather brought old ones to the surface. London's growing black population had always believed that they were harrassed by a police force which was not sensitive to their particular needs. The riots in Brixton in 1981 showed not only that the Met had lost the confidence of the black community, but also that it seemed unable to respond to civil unrest with discipline. In 1985, Broadwater Farm, and Brixton again, showed tht not just tension but almost hatred existed between the police and the black community. Then in 1986, in a case that shocked Londoners to the core, it was revealed that, in 1983, policemen from a van patrolling in north London had viciously beaten up a group of youngsters. Thirty policemen had then taken vows of silence so that the culprits could not be found. A short but outraged press campaign forced the Met to get to grips with the case, and some policemen were eventually charged with the offence.

To this catalogue of dissatisfaction, the Met replies that something between 66% and 75% of all Londoners express satisfaction with its performance – though other surveys have found much lower figures. And senior officers of the Met say, this time with more justification, that they are aware of the shortcomings in the force and determined to do something about them.

The essential problem of the Met is that, unlike all other police forces in Britain, it is not responsible to any local authority. The "police authority" for the Met is the Home Secretary, an anomaly justified on the grounds that the Met's functions include such matters as diplomatic protection, guarding the Royal family, and running the Special Branch, which is the executive arm of the security services. All these are said to be national, not local, functions. Thus, the theory goes, the Met must be accountable to a national politician. The reasoning is spurious. The vast majority of the Met's establishment is in local police stations doing the kind of job done by policemen all over the country. In any event, to look to the Home Secretary – of any colour – for a serious attempt to improve the performance of the Met is worse than useless. The law-and-order vote is the easiest to get, and lose, in the whole of British politics. Thus Labour Home Secretaries, frightened of being accused of being soft on crime, do nothing to keep the Met in line; Tory Home Secretaries have no real wish to criticise the Met at all, but even if they did, are too scared by the hang-'em-flog-'em wing of their party to do anything of the sort.

The professionalism and competence of the Met thus depends crucially on the performance and character of its chief officer, the Commissioner. For the last 14 years the Met has been run by three extraordinary men. From 1972 to 1977, the Commissioner was Sir Robert Mark, a scholarly man, much given to lecturing the public on crime and its causes, and an unrivalled scourge of corruption. He needed to be; the Met in the early 1970s was rotten to the core. Many of its specialist squads – the Flying Squad, the Drugs Squad, the team that dealt with the sex industry in Soho – had become hopelessly compromised. Mark cleaned up the force as well as any man could. He was succeeded by a bluff Scot. Sir David McNee was much more of a conventional copper – hard, uncompromising, and loath to see his men shackled or criticised. His annual reports were miles away from the elegant erudition of Mark (one started: "The highlight of the year was the wedding of His Royal Highness Prince Charles . . . it was a spectacular and happy occasion . . ."). He was a professional policeman of the highest order, but the Met needed more than someone prepared to defend his officers through thick and thin. On his retirement in 1982 it was widely considered that he had been something of a failure.

In his place came the present Commissioner, Sir Kenneth Newman, one of the most fascinating men in London. A man who started his career in Palestine, and has run the police in Ulster, is bound to be tough. He is a small soft-spoken man with sticky-out ears, but with eyes that can terrify. And he is very, very clever. A senior civil servant once told me that Newman had a better grasp of the complexities of modern management and finance than any Whitehall permanent secretary; his reports are almost works of academic scholarship.

The goal that Newman has set himself is straightforward; it is to reprofessionalise the Met so that it becomes a force of which Londoners can feel proud. Among his top staff he engenders remarkable loyalty and devotion; among many of his coppers he is a good deal less popular. When his plans for a new professionalism were first unveiled, one of his senior officers has said, the stations were full of "canteen lizards spitting venom" at the mention of his name.

The reason for his unpopularity is that the culture of the Met is unique – quite different, policemen from outside London never tire of saying, from that of other forces. The Met is a self-contained band of outsiders; only about 30% of its establishment are Londoners. It has its own argot, and its own values. As the important 1983 report by the Policy Studies Institute on the policing of London showed, the Met is imbued with a male, chauvinist, casually racist, heavy-drinking, macho set of values which are not those which any longer appeal to most Londoners. Newman has set out to change all that. The Met, he believes, can only do its job if it polices with the consent of the public. That means that his men have to drop some of the attitudes that they have come to regard as an essential part of a good copper. And the Commissioner has had to try to introduce this change of climate in the force when it has been under attack – and some at least of that attack has been justified – from many left-wing politicians in London. Black politicians, in particular, frankly disbelieve that the Met can be reformed without some clear public accountability for its actions. They are joined, more and more, by middle-class parents who have been appalled at the heavy-handed treatment that the Met hands out to youngsters. Things cannot continue as they are; no serious attempt to restructure the government of the city can ignore the need to find some trust in those who are meant to keep its peace.

9
BEATING ON

When the United Nations was set up in New York in 1945, the world's pundits saw the new skyscraper on the East River as a symbol of the passing of power. The League of Nations had been at Geneva; here was proof that the ways of the old world had passed. For the next 20 years as the pax Americana settled on Europe, they seemed to have been proved right.

Times move on. We are now mad about the Pacific basin, the technological skill of the Japanese, and the awakening of China. To believe some of the Jeremiahs, poor Europe has been left behind – "Europessimism" has been coined as a term to catch the mood of gloom.

Yet at the same time as the economic and cultural focus of the world is said to have shifted away from Europe, so the internationalisation of affluence has made it the destination for millions of Americans and Japanese, searching for a cultural climate distinct from that back home. Quite apart from tourism, the European economy is hardly derisory. At 1985 prices and exchange rates, the USA had a gross domestic product of $3,865 billion, Japan one of $1,308 billion, and the countries of the EEC (including Spain and Portugal) $2,406 billion. The EEC is the most populous of these three trading blocks; it has about 320m people compared with about 235m in the USA and 119m in Japan. The people of Europe still enjoy a remarkably high life-style, and their economies have grown at historically high rates since 1945.

Of economics . . .

Britain's people and its economy have shared in this
prosperity. Yet it is trite economics to say that the country
has lagged behind its European partners. Britain's
economy has grown by only about 80% since the late
1950s, since when those of France and Germany have
more than doubled their output. National income per
head in Britain is now way below that of France,
Germany and the Nordic countries, and according to the
most recent figures, below that of Italy too. Britons have
less cars and television sets than Italians; less telephones
than the French. When they travel, according to a
much-cited article in the *New York Times* in 1985, they
use cardboard suitcases, and look a bedraggled bunch
compared with their European cousins – never mind
their American ones. According to both figures and the
testimony of those who wish Britain no ill, the country
has become a poor one.

London is thus the capital of a nation which has been
in seeming decline for 30 years. But it doesn't feel like it.
This isn't just because London is the richest part of
Britain, though anyone who has spent ten minutes in
London and half-an-hour out of it knows that it is. Nor is
it simply because – as we have seen – London is the most
internationally-minded part of Britain, though that is
important. London has a greater willingness to accept
foreign food, has more foreign tourists, more immigrants,
and an economy one of whose key parts, the City, is
geared to a world market. Londoners have discovered
how to enjoy themselves in high-quality, low-cost leisure
activities in just the way the French and Italians did years
ago.

The key point is rather different. I think that London,
uniquely among European cities, has discovered –
perhaps I should hedge a bit – is on the verge of
discovering, a unique cultural personality that takes the
best of American go-for-it classlessness, places it in a
quintessentially historic European city, and mixes it with

the phlegm and good humour of Britain at its best. And this cultural personality, never forget, has the world language of the twenty-first century – English – as its mother tongue.

Now comes the punt. I believe that this less than ten-year-old mixture is potentially an economic winner. In the street-cred economy, where the new mood is most evident, London is without question the centre of European economic activity. No other capital has such a critical mass of creative people in music, fashion, art, advertising, food and drink, broadcasting, film, and design. If the qualities that have made London so successful in these sectors can make their presence felt in finance, software, the law, education – all businesses whose product will be instantly tradeable abroad by telephone or satellite within a decade – then London's service industries should be set for expansion.

Then there is tourism. There is no reason whatsoever why London's tourist boom should come to an end. Granted, the industry needs to wake up a little – most of the mid-1980s boom was more because of the $/£ exchange rate than because tourism companies went out of their way to market a product with flair. But in an increasingly affluent and interconnected world, and one where the price of oil looks set to stay low for some time, the numbers of those who want holidays away from their home town should continue to grow. London can, and should, make it its business to grab an ever bigger share of this market.

Add in dockland. Not everything there will work; the Stolport is a big gamble, Canary Wharf a bigger one. The LDDC has convinced few, as yet, that it can work in the Royal Docks the same magic as it has applied further west. But in general the prospects are good, mainly because the LDDC has been able to come along with its sweeteners at precisely the same time that the transport infrastructure in east London is finally getting built.

The M25 is likely to be a further growth point. True, the

road was built without any clear idea of whether it was meant to be a by-pass around London or a site for development on its fringe. There are those who say it cannot do both; that if the development comes, the road will be unable to cope (there are some alarming estimates of the impact of the Channel Tunnel on the eastern sector of the M25). But in some key areas – like the stretch between the M3 and the M40, in the west, and at the Dartford Tunnel in the east – those pressures can be resolved, without any major environmental loss, by widening the M25 to four lanes.

Taken together, these developments give more than a glimmer of hope for a bright economic recovery. But all this could easily be killed before it has reached infancy. It could, for example, be ruined if the still-stuffy British establishment fails to invest in the industries of tomorrow, and continues to put its cash into an ever-overheating property market. It could be diverted if politicians decide that London must rebuild what some of them like to call its "traditional" manufacturing industries. These well-meaning folk forget that those industries had only 50 years in the sun, and that nowhere in London – and few places in Britain – will ever again be able to offer investors a comparative advantage in many manufacturing processes.

Worst of all, the new London economy could turn out to be no more than a glossy apple with a maggot at its core. The maggot would be an under-class, poorly educated, highly politicised, badly housed, often black, excluded from any prospect of economic prosperity. That would be more than tragic; it would be dangerous. It is why there is a desperate need to improve the skills and education of young Londoners, house them better, police them more sensitively, and, above all, offer them equal opportunities, whatever their colour.

Politics ...

How much does politics matter to London's economics? As far as the local scene is concerned, the borough councils have three key areas; in planning, housing, and race relations. In planning, the councils must tread a difficult tightrope. It is of the utmost importance to London's largest industry – tourism – that the historic aspect of the city is preserved. The conservationists must be heeded; there can be no more disasters like the South Bank arts complex, a lump of concrete stretching along one of the finest parts of the river. At the same time, the councils must do all they can to encourage new small businesses into the centre of town. That means that they should preserve the outer shell of London's old buildings, but take a relaxed view of what goes on inside them – retailing, office work, small service industries, even light manufacturing.

In housing, the councils must be prepared to enfranchise the tenants in their estates. They should welcome private capital, make some estates over to those who live in them, and look for more opportunities for the housing associations to play a role. On race relations, the councils must give a clear lead. They need to be equal opportunity employers while many of London's private-sector firms patently are not, and they should keep the pressure on those firms to change their ways. London is, now and for ever, a multi-racial city.

The problems are different in education. The ILEA is now approaching a crisis. If many more middle-class parents desert the system for the private sector, the ILEA will be left looking after sink schools, staffed by bad teachers, turning out disaffected pupils. More money cannot be the answer, so long as most of it would go straight into the pockets of those teachers who have failed to stretch children to their full ability. The task for the ILEA now is to look kindly on parent-power, to try to get a much greater diversity in its schools, to go openly for excellence (perhaps by setting up some "magnet" schools which cater unashamedly for the brightest) and to do all it can to convince London's affluent parents that the state system can serve their needs.

The problem with this catalogue of action is obvious. Conservative politicians are more likely to be persuaded of the need for action on housing and education. Labour ones have been far more innovative on race, and probably have a better grasp of the connection between conservation and economic prosperity. So what will the future political map of London look like?

Some inkling of that can be gleaned from looking at the figures for general elections since October 1974, when the Labour Party last won an overall majority in the House of Commons. In that election, Labour and the Conservatives polled within 13,000 votes of each other in the 57 outer London constituencies. The Conservatives had 40.2% of the vote, and won 35 seats; Labour had 39.7% of the vote, and won 22. Five years later, at the time of Mrs Thatcher's first triumph, the picture changed. The Tories had 48.9% of the votes for 40 seats; Labour 36.1% for 17. But it was 1983 that saw the real collapse. The Tory share actually fell, to 47.6%, but the party won 44 seats. Labour's vote collapsed, to 25.7% for their 11 seats. In all of outer London, Labour polled less than 3,000 votes more than the Alliance (who, thanks to Britain's quirky electoral laws, won no seats at all). Put another way, in less than ten years, Labour lost over 300,000 votes in the suburbs.

Now take inner London. In October 1974, Labour won 52.9% of the votes and 29 of the seats. The Tories had 31.4% of the vote, and won 6 seats. In 1983, the Labour vote declined to 47.2%, and they won only 25 seats; the Conservatives' 39.9% netted 10. Again, it was 1983 that saw the real change. Then Labour won only 38.6% of the votes for 15 seats; the Conservatives won 35.9% for 12 seats; and the Alliance won 22.8% for 2 seats. Labour, in inner London, lost 170,000 votes between 1979 and 1983. In the whole of London in 1974 it had 8 seats more than the Conservatives; in 1983, 30 seats less.

Is this a secular change, or is it a cyclical one? In other words, will Labour, ever regain its position? Granted, the Conservatives are unlikely to do as well at the next general election as they did in 1983, but that does not necessarily mean that Labour will benefit. The Alliance is almost bound to be a more potent threat in 1987 or 1988 than it was in 1983; it will quite possibly pick up a few outer London seats from the Conservatives, and it is not beyond the bounds of reason that it will gain one or two from Labour. But inner London will almost certainly continue to support Labour more than any other party. I would be surprised beyond words if the new, directly elected ILEA that has replaced the old GLC sub-committee did not have a Labour majority for the rest of the century. That means that as long as the ILEA continues in being, any changes in London's schools are going to have to be imposed by central government.

It means, also, that most inner-London boroughs will usually be run by the Labour Party. If Labour does not win a majority at the next election, some of those boroughs, and some Labour ILEA councillors, will try once more to set up an alternative, left-wing city government in London in just the same way Ken Livingstone did with the GLC; and the policies of such councillors might be more left-wing than Livingstone followed. That would be bad for London's schools, housing and businesses.

It need not happen. The London Labour Party is approaching a historic crossroads. The years from 1981 to 1986 were given over, in part, to play and posture politics. But long before the end of the GLC that mood was changing. The rhetoric was abandoned, and Ken and his chums got down to some serious work. There was the glimmer of a chance in the last 18 months of the GLC that the ruling clique round Livingstone had realised that it was possible both to encourage enterprise and entrepreneurship in the city, and to pursue their distinctive social policies.

The question now is whether the London Labour Party retreats into a left-wing laager, or whether its young and unquestionably able councillors develop a pragmatic socialism. That would be one that combines good housekeeping (which will mean they will have to take on the public-sector unions), the encouragement of private enterprise, and the appreciation that vast municipal empires running housing and education help nobody – least of all the people whom Labour thinks it has a historic duty to protect. On balance, I'm optimistic enough to think they will go for the pragmatism.

It would, in any event, be quite wrong to give the impression that the political problems of London's future are solely within the province of the Labour Party. They are not. The Conservative government made a complete hash of abolishing the GLC. On balance, the decision was the right one, as the GLC had spent 20 years looking vainly for a role, and the politics of fun which Livingstone bequeathed it were not sufficient justification for its cost. But the government had never thought the problem through. They had to backtrack on the ILEA (where they agreed to set up direct elections); they found that they had to institute a joint board of borough nominees for fire protection; and they left so much unfinished business in 1986 that a London Residuary Body (*sic*) is trying to decide what to do with the GLC's land, its debt, some of its staff, and its research.

Meanwhile, the boroughs are meant to co-operate on planning decisions, waste disposal, and voluntary organisations – where the GLC did much of its most important work – while the Department of Transport takes over the strategic road network. The Arts Council, just to complete the picture, will run the South Bank arts complex.

It is much too early to say how this will shake out, save to say that it is unlikely to save money for a few years (though the government massaged the figures in 1986 so that each of the London boroughs could cut its rates). In some cases, the Tories have been so keen to show any savings at all that they have foolishly starved the GLC's successors of much-needed cash. The board that will run the South Bank for the Arts Council, for instance, has some great ideas for making the wasteland fun, but they will need far more money than the government has yet given them to see their plans through.

Conservatives are also to blame for failing to reform the Metropolitan Police. London is becoming a violent city. Some of its sink estates are riddled with heroin, crimes of violence have increased, and sexual offences have risen sharply (much more sharply than official figures suggest). Meanwhile, the productivity of the Met in terms of crime cleared up has declined, and it has suffered a catastrophic loss of confidence among blacks, young people and their parents. And all the Conservative government can do is to pay the police more, promise them lots of lovely new equipment, and treat anyone who dares criticise them like a Communist caught strangling his granny.

The problem of the Met will not be solved until it is rendered accountable to politicians who believe that they can make some political capital out of criticising it. National politicians will never do that; some local politicians might. There is an outside chance that if the Met had to justify itself, for example, to some of London's black politicians – in genuinely powerful forums, not just in the consultative committees that have been in place for the last few years – it would learn more about the needs of the black community, and blacks would learn that not all in the police have horns and a tail. What is true beyond peradventure is that no other system of controlling the Met stands as great a chance of improving both its productivity and its standing with the public.

Should the body to which the Met is accountable be a reborn GLC? Will the shambles left in the GLC's wake become so unbearable that some future government will have to reinvent it? Well . . . who knows? Some argue that the boroughs will never agree on anything in the GLC's absence; others say that it was the threat of the GLC descending on them like a great hammer that made the boroughs unco-operative. Once the GLC is out of the way, in this view, all will be sweetness and light. Don't expect it to happen for a while.

One idea whose time will surely come is not a new GLC, but a new structure for the boroughs. The economic and social problems that some of the Crescent boroughs now face are clearly beyond their abilities or resources. That raises the possibility that when the Boundaries Commission starts to look at the boroughs in 1987 it will quickly decide that some amalgamation is necessary. Various schemes are around; I have heard five, ten and twelve big boroughs suggested, and London will not have 32 in the next century. The proponents of amalgamations are particularly keen to merge inner with outer boroughs; that way, they say, burdens will be shared.

Others doubt whether this makes sense. Some boroughs already include both rich and poor areas (Hounslow and Kensington & Chelsea, for instance) and their record suggests that policy is set mainly to help the rich parts. Again, it is objected that mergers would destroy a natural community. But that claims too much for the present boroughs. They are only 20 years old, and their boundaries in no way coincide with the ten distinct regions of London that I have been using in this book. In any event, the concept of community can be overdone. As Londoners become more affluent, more of them will live in three, four, or five places throughout their lives in the city. Their communities will be their friends – and their friends might live in any part of London.

... and philosophy

That's a taste of the politics and economics of the London of the future. As for its philosophy, its heart, that depends on its people. The key to understanding London is to recognise that Londoners have built a new city twice in the last 40 years. The first reconstruction was after Hitler; the second, not yet appreciated, was when they took what had become the epitome of the worst of England – puritan, stuffy, politically staid, bureaucratic, class-ridden – and made of it one of the great cities of the world. A city that, as Paul Theroux accurately said, is in many ways a country of its own. London is in Britain but not of it. It belongs to all the world.

There is no other great city of the west that offers so many contrasts, so many delightful places to live, so much safety, so much solidity, so much change, so much fun, so much intellect, so much soul. And where's the heart of this beating town? Not in Piccadilly; not in Leicester Square; not in Westminster or Whitehall. It's where the heart always is; at home, in the 2.3m households in the city, where the 6.7m people who live there go about their usual tasks – every so often, if they are wise, pinching themselves to check that they are lucky enough to live in such a place, at such a time.